Elsie &
The Pentecostals

Janice Rasmussen
Ron Johnson

Golden Calf
Books

Published by Golden Calf Books

ISBN 979-8-9897093-0-4

Cover Art Concept: Ron Johnson
Cover Art Designer: Marko Mirkovic

Typesetting services by BOOKOW.COM

Contents

Part I

Roy

ST PATRICK'S DAY 1957

Six days a week, the stuffy Redondo Avenue dance hall is a place of sin. On the seventh day, it transforms into a church—Roy Rasmussen's church. Nothing changes but the name. The haggard men and women seated inside resemble their surroundings: unwashed, thrown together, rented. That doesn't matter to Pastor Roy—he wants sinners like them. Why preach to the choir?

He's already into his morning sermon, having wrapped the song service ten minutes ago. Song service is where Roy shines—he spent years on the road singing hymns with his wife Elsie, currently seated at the piano behind him. Sermons were never his strong suit and now boredom's creeping in to the sinners. Fortunately, Pentecostals like Roy have a solution for that: *tongues*. Wild, flapping tongues, speaking the divine language of the Holy Spirit. Roy's tongue will fly at the sermon's grand finale, but for now he's focused on the message: Jesus Christ has come to save you.

As the sermon continues, bleary eyes are wiped. Mouths yawn. Roy changes course, raising his voice to drive the sermon heavy. The friendly Christian offer of salvation turns to condemnation: decline Jesus and suffer the consequence. Roy's sharp voice bounces off the walls of the stuffy dance hall. Carefree sinner attitudes have thickened—he's straightened 'em out but now they need a payoff. The Holy Spirit stirs inside of Roy—tongues are imminent. The end is near.

A bright flash from the corner catches Roy's eye. He looks to the flash but it slides away. More flashes appear. Light fills the dance hall—the church is sparkling. Roy's head suddenly fills with extreme pressure—it's about to pop. He lurches heavily over the pulpit, eyes askew and unfocused. Elsie sees her husband struggling and knows something's wrong.

"Don't you people see him?" Roy points to the rear, "Jesus is there in the corner —look in the light!"

The sinners twist around in their chairs but see nothing. They hold their breath: *Is this part of the show?*

"Elsie, I'm blind!"

Roy collapses to the floor. Church elders—Roy's most trusted men—rush to the pulpit, but he can't be raised. They quickly load him into a car for transport to nearby Bethany Chapel, home of the mighty Prophet David Schoch. That's where he'll be treated—hands and prayers heal all.

The elders screech to a stop outside Bethany Chapel, rushing inside to request the Prophet's healing. The Prophet races out to the waiting car. Roy's eldest daughter Lana watches from the back seat as Prophet Schoch and the elders lay hands on the slumped body of her dad. The men pray loudly—unapologetically—for healing. Pentecostal tongues rise to the heavens.

* * *

In our small apartment, my brothers and I watch my favorite cartoon: Popeye and Bluto. Dad left for church three hours ago, leaving me in charge of four-year-old Mark and ten-year-old Gilbert, who is sick. I'm Janice—eleven years old—and I thought it very unusual for dad to let us stay home from church. Maybe he wasn't feeling well either, or maybe he was just softening. He'd finally taken us off the never-ending road of evangelism to chart a normal life here in Long Beach—a life of stability and television viewing. We even managed to complete a full year of school without leaving for a new town. Life for young children is good.

The front door explodes open with church men carrying dad's weak body. They shuffle past me and deposit dad on the couch. I watch him moan in agony.

"Jesus, heal me. Jesus, heal me," he mumbles over and over.

Mom arrives, falling to her knees and telling dad she loves him—that he's going to be alright. I know something's terribly wrong and start crying.

The men pray over Roy's limp body on the couch. Their combined voices grow louder; they know if they make a louder din—give more glory to God—the chance of a miracle increases. But given Roy's dire condition, they also know *something extra* is needed for this miracle to occur. They need the Prayer Warrior—they need big Evelyn.

Three-hundred-fifty pound Evelyn Rasmussen, married to dad's brother Albin, was a mighty lady preacher in the church world—a *big gun* in the holy roller terms of

Pentecostalism. She and Albin evangelized on the Jesus circuit just as we had for the last couple years, but Albin & Evelyn were far better at it. Especially Evelyn.

The church men's *something extra* arrives as Evelyn walks into the apartment, a whoosh of air carrying behind her. The men step aside.

"Leave him, Satan!" she growls. Her powerful hands wrap around dad's arm. "Get out of this man, Devil!"

Evelyn cocks her head to the church men, "Place his feet up like Elijah the Prophet!" The men move quickly, straightening dad's legs on the couch and placing a pillow under his feet. Evelyn leans over Roy's weak body and begins her Pentecostal tongue gibberish, howling and bucking like a wounded animal as frothy spit collects like cake frosting at the corners of her mouth.

I watch the Pentecostal circus unfold as precious time ticks away. Can't these idiots understand that my dad needs a hospital, and quickly?

"Get up, Roy. You will stand *now*, Roy. Stand and be healed!"

Evelyn's butt sticks in my face while she barks instructions to my dying father. I feel a strong urge to smack it but want no attention from these gross old loonies in our apartment. I'm eleven—they must be in their hundreds.

After a torturous hour of prayers and barking, dad's condition hasn't improved. Something terrible has blinded him and he's barely breathing. Finally realizing how dire the situation is, church man Don Whelan pulls the plug on the magic act and instructs Evelyn to call an ambulance.

In 1957, apartment building telephones operated on a 'party line' system, meaning multiple people could be on the line at once. If you had an emergency, you had to cut in and make your request. Evelyn cuts in heavy:

"We need an ambulance at 435 Walnut. Come quick, a man is dying!"

Ten long minutes pass before ambulance men enter our apartment. They immediately recognize how serious dad's condition is, loading him on a stretcher and moving as one to the front door. Dad's arm catches on the door jamb; the ambulance driver deftly folds it across his chest and exits. The ambulance takes off down the street with sirens wailing. I run behind, screaming.

Dad was two miles from the Veteran's Hospital when he fell at 11am. At Bethany Chapel, that distance was four miles. From our apartment, five. In their impassioned drive to save Roy with prayer, the loonies drove him further from healing. It took a full four hours before he arrived at the hospital.

* * *

Dusk approaches. I've spent the last couple hours alone in dad's car, crying and begging Jesus to heal him. In our apartment, my brother Gilbert bargains with Jesus: a lifetime of tithing in exchange for dad's life. I've not seen dad or mom for hours now. Exhausted and hungry, I leave the car and head inside. "Dad will be okay," I assure myself. *He'll be home tonight.*

I tune back in to my favorite cartoon: Popeye and Bluto's eternal struggle for Olive Oyl. Dad's cousin Lyle walks in and says mom wants to see me next door in the Huska family's apartment—dad's distant relatives. I walk across the porch to their door and hear unsettling sounds coming from inside. Shaky nerves unsettle me.

I enter the apartment to a room full of crying, moaning adults speaking tongue gibberish. They wring their hands—peeking through their fingers at me—awaiting the moment when mom's shaky voice tells me dad's in heaven with Jesus.

My young brain tries to process the day's events. It's only been a couple hours since dad was taken to the hospital: How could he get to Heaven so fast? Did he fly?

The room falls silent except for weeping Aunt Evelyn, the mighty Prayer Warrior who'd failed to cast the devil out of dad. Eunice Lenning, dad's cousin by marriage, sees my distress and rushes over to put hands on my head. She hums—the buildup to tongue talking—but it only makes me feel worse and I want her to stop. What she's doing is stupid and won't change anything. My dad is dead.

I look over at mom and see Mark sitting with her. I can tell he's confused, hungry, and sleepy. Mark was at the hospital with mom and knew dad was sick, but at four years old, he doesn't understand *dead.*

Gilbert arrives for similar treatment: Prayers, hands, and staring. Our older sister Lana was fortunate to be among cousins when news was delivered to her at Bethany Chapel—the church where dad was first brought for healing.

Dad's death that night came from a brain aneurysm. Police were called to the hospital—standard procedure when a 34-year-old man dies under strange circumstances. They spoke with mom and cleared her name. The church people were lucky I wasn't at the hospital: I would have told the police everything about these lunatics and their healing shenanigans. They all had blood on their hands.

Once things quiet down in the apartment, Albin speaks: "Let's take an offering for Elsie and the family," he requests for the new widow, 34-year-old Elsie Rasmussen.

Albin grabs a pillow from the sofa to pass around. Adults in the room reach deep into empty pockets as the pillow circles toward them. Elsie—mom—stares vacantly from the sofa.

The Rasmussen clan consisted of two daughters and seven sons, of which dad was the baby. Dad was closest to his brother Albin; they were the only two Rasmussens lit with the furious fire of Pentecostalism. I despised Albin for many reasons, past, present, and future—to my disgust, he was now taking charge.

The sofa pillow arrives back to Albin. Gilbert—always untrusting of Uncle Albin —eyes the offering as Albin counts it out: twenty-four bucks and loose change. The gathered relatives are impressed by the sum. Big smiles paint their faces as they present the offering to my shell-shocked mom.

Our relatives surely loved my dad and meant well. Now that he's gone, non-church business needs attention. Telephone calls are placed to our fragmented roots in Minnesota and Michigan, and to South Dakota where the Rasmussen clan is notified. All their crying and yakking made me desperate to flee the room. To be away from them all. Anywhere but there.

I stayed that night with Albin & Evelyn, crawling into bed with my older cousin Joann. I lay awake the entire night—all thoughts on dad. Where was he sleeping? Was this real? Would it all go away in the morning?

Pastor Roy Rasmussen

GOOD MEMORIES FADE AWAY

In Long Beach—when dad was alive—we were a happy family. Our previous life was constant turmoil: a pitiful collection of lived-in cars, freezing farmhouses, food handouts, and the ever-present Pentecostalism. I was always hungry and cold. In Long Beach, the sun rose for us every day—until it didn't.

Long Beach life felt good and I was happy to see dad at home for once. Even though he never paid much attention to me, I began to feel like he cared. Before Long Beach, he was always running out the door somewhere; Now he only ran down the street to pastor his ad-hoc church—the rented dance hall on Redondo Avenue. Maybe dad felt age creeping in and slowed down to get out of the un-productive race to save sinners' souls. I like to imagine he was planning to settle down and take care of his family, to give all of us more love while continuing to love Jesus—a fair pursuit.

Our initial arrival to Long Beach on October 18, 1956, was still dicey given our itinerant lifestyle. We had no furniture, and most of our possessions existed in paper bags packed in the trunk of dad's car. Bibles, Fuller Brush leftovers, and cleaning supplies. Bedding, sacks of clothes, and ragged pajamas. Mom still had her accordion but dad's guitar was gone—accidentally run over as we left Wichita.

Thankfully, dad's double-cousin Fred Lenning directed us to the fourplex apart-ment building where his sisters lived. With John Huska's family across from us and Helmer Gunderson's family next door, we now had cousins to replace the cold isolation of our previous life. The apartment was even furnished—we'd live large.

Our apartment had a pull-down bed in the living room where dad and mom slept. Down a little hallway was a bedroom where the four of us slept on twin beds: Mark and Gilbert in one, me and Lana in the other. This may seem cramped to outsiders but we were used to it after coming from a 27-foot trailer in Wichita, and that didn't even have a toilet. We lived better than ever and were happy to finally be somewhere good.

Hopeful in Long Beach before dad died

Dad wanted to hold church services immediately and found a dance hall at the corner of Redondo & Anaheim offering cheap Sunday rent. He'd rise early on Sunday to sweep away the filth left by Saturday night's rowdy crowd of drinkers & smokers, transforming the hall into a makeshift church.

Since Sunday was basically charity work, dad still needed to earn money. His brother Albin—the uncle we knew all too well from Wichita—had connections to a waterless cookware company and got dad onboard. This was a big deal for us: Dad finally had a real job and regular paycheck. We started living like normal people, and we loved our parents even if they remained distant to us.

I fondly remember sitting at the table in our apartment's tiny kitchenette, watching dad cook me breakfast: Cream of Wheat with buttered toast. That was my earliest memory of love for him, and the feeling that he might even love me back. Seeing him peaceful—not running out the door to some tent meeting or screaming about Jesus in a rural church—was wonderful. A weary thought crossed my mind: Why wasn't it always like this? Why did dad have to put us through so much pain?

We were the new kids in school for the umpteenth time. Gilbert entered 5th grade, I entered 6th, and Lana started Junior High. Mark was still too young for school so he stayed home with mom.

Gilbert and I went to Burbank Elementary, eight blocks from our apartment. We walked to school together every day, peeking in shop windows along Fourth Street.

Many times we'd see dad and mom drive by on their way for morning coffee at the Park Pantry, their favorite restaurant. They never waved—I guess they didn't see us.

I was so shy at school that during lunch hour I'd hide behind a door and talk to my imaginary friend. Lunch was a fried egg sandwich or thermos of cream corn —meals I'd long since grown accustomed to. I soon opened up to my classmates, learning baton twirling, doing back bends, and pretending to be in a marching band. I even played hop scotch with other kids.

During these happy times, Gilbert and I had a *Shopping News* paper route and felt pretty important earning our little paycheck. We rolled up our papers and walked our routes, sticking them in door handles and mail slots. We were pretty jazzed at our earnings: $5 total, split evenly down the middle. I could hardly wait to spend my half, heading down to the corner store to splurge on candy. I was smart to spend mine quick: Gilbert saved his, only to have dad borrow it and never pay him back.

Long Beach life still had its low points. Since dancing was strictly forbidden by Pentecostals, dad and mom kept me out of the school's square dance. While other kids joined arms and innocently skipped around, I was forced to watch from the sidelines. For Jesus.

Another low point was when dad's mom—our beloved Grandma Matilda—died in January 1957. Dad and Albin wanted to take their wives on a car run out to South Dakota for the funeral, leaving the kids behind under the care of seventh-grader Lana and older cousin Joann. Mom and Evelyn were furious with the plan and refused to go. The men drove alone to Bruce, South Dakota, in the middle of blizzard season, where on arrival they learned the ground was too frozen for burial. Grandma's body had to be stored until warm weather arrived to thaw the ground.

A couple months before his death, dad flew to Denver, Colorado, for a cookware company meeting. Our future looked good now, and I loved him for it. We headed to LAX to pick him up after the meeting and I was excited to see him in his new red tie. Rasmussen men weren't the most attractive but dad was one of the better ones: He had curly hair and Midwestern charm, played guitar and sang tunes. The main thing detracting from his appearance was the blinking eye—the one that worsened over the years.

When dad got off the plane, he ran to the car with a skip in his step. I was impressed knowing that this was my dad and I was his daughter. He was working—earning a real paycheck—and for once we had food on a regular basis. I was so proud of him.

TORN APART

It's been three days since dad died. I don't know where mom is but I know where Gilbert is—with me under Albin's control. Albin's taking us to the mortuary to view dad's body, something I don't want to do. I ask why we have to see him before the funeral; Albin says it's to show respect—as if dad would even know or care. It makes no sense to me but Albin's in charge and if I give him trouble he'll put me in deeper trouble with mom—wherever she is.

Gilbert and I load into the backseat of dad's '54 Bel Air—Albin snatched it for himself—and begin the short drive to Mottels & Peak Mortuary, just around the corner from our Walnut Ave apartment. I stare through the rear window—the same window where I'd spent so much of my young life counting stars while dad and mom drove cross-country spreading the gospel. I long for that innocent window to return, but I know it can't—those days are gone now. My nerves twirl in anticipation of viewing dad's body. My tummy hurts.

We arrive at the mortuary. I expect to see mom but I can't find her and that scares me. Albin grabs my arm to guide me through the door, rather roughly I think. It feels like he wants to shove me through the door—maybe he knows I'll tell on him one day.

Inside, the funeral director escorts us into a sterile-looking holding area to await the mortician. A man enters the room walking oddly—no heel, all toes. His lapel tag proclaims him *Mr Hess–Mortician and Dresser*. He sports a big nose and sticky black hair parted tight down the middle. Mr Hess whispers a greeting to us and we whisper back. He offers a limp handshake, though I see his hands are strong and firm—each fingernail polished to a shine. It's all too weird and I feel a big scream building inside my chest.

Mr Hess escorts us to the viewing room where dad's body lies in a casket. The deathly silent room is filled with the odor of carnations mixed with vinegar and disinfectant. Mr Hess motions towards dad's casket, "Oh, he looks like he's sleeping."

I peek in the casket to see dad's head resting on a white satin pillow, hands folded across his chest. He's dressed in the only suit he owned—the tattered one with the red tie—and looks like he's going to church or a business meeting. His swollen face smiles which really bothers me. He looks like my doll at home—as if he'd come from another planet. I notice something wrong with his hairline, like he's been scalped and put back together again. His lips and eyes are shut tight but a white substance seeps out of them. I ask Albin about it and he tells me morticians use a special glue on dead people so they won't suddenly open their eyes. My brain races, trying to figure out what else Mr Hess did to my dad.

Gilbert is far braver than me, seeming to enjoy the clinical aspect of seeing a body. I hear him sniff around the casket, trying to make out the strange odor permeating the room. He reaches in the casket to touch dad's hands. "They're real hard and cold," he reports.

I know I'll have to view dad's body again at the funeral, and that angers me—how stupid is Albin to make me do this twice? But Albin's my boss now and I have to obey him. I look forward to the day when I'm older and he loses power over me. Albin is wicked and deserves punishment; I don't want him to be my uncle anymore.

The room's odor, the strange mortician, dad's otherworldly body—all of it overloads my emotions and shuts them down. I suddenly notice mom in our presence and that soothes me. Gilbert and I watch her caress dad's hair and cry out with terrible sadness. I wish I could join her in grief, but I'm too numb to cry.

Afterwards, Albin takes us to McDonald's on Long Beach Boulevard for a meal. Our appetites are gone so we nibble at burgers and fries while trying to forget what we saw. Mom isn't with us, she's retreated to the care of the same Pentecostal goofballs who took an active role in dad's death. Little Mark is with mom and the Pentecostals; Our big sister Lana—the family ghost—is nowhere to be found.

Albin's wife Evelyn—the mighty Prayer Warrior—takes me downtown to replace second-hand clothes with new ones for the funeral. I choose a pretty pink dress with matching gloves and purse, but the dress requires a bra—something I've never worn before. Aunt Evelyn is an enormous torpedo-breasted woman who surely knows how a bra works, but she's also famous in our church world and I'm uncomfortable asking her for help. Without mom around, my hand is forced. I ask the Prayer Warrior for help—two minutes later I'm wearing my first bra.

Funeral Day

Pentecostal Funeral

Friday, 11am. I sit in a mortuary pew across from dad's casket, fighting the urge to stare at his smiling face. I try being brave, but my nerves act up again in the face of uncertainty.

Friends and relatives file by the casket, gasping in shock at seeing dad for the first time. Dad's cousin Fred Lenning limps past; I knew Fred from our horrible years on the road: He was the man directing dad's travels, the shady Pentecostal shot-caller with a chronic limp that Jesus refused to heal.

Fred approaches me, leaning down within earshot. "Your daddy's in Heaven and not suffering anymore," he reassures me through sour breath. "You'll see him again one day." Fred's words confuse me, because if dad's in Heaven, why is he lying right there in the casket?

Other relatives visit me to deliver their reassuring nonsense. I don't like any of them but they insist on liking me, and I wonder why they feel so compelled to reassure me of Heaven. I realize it's what Pentecostals say when there's no explanation for Jesus allowing a young father to die in front of his children. It's what they say to children who spent hours begging Jesus to heal their dad, children who believed their dad would come home—children whose prayers went unanswered. These people want the funeral—and the events of the preceding days—to be as painless as possible for *themselves*. To do that, they pay lip service to fatherless children.

Lyle Lenning begins the service with a fond remembrance of Roy—his cousin and pal. I also knew Lyle from our previous life and he was a nice man, much like dad —an honest and faithful rube. Lyle talks about their long friendship and how they were buddies in the Army and at North Central Bible School. He shares stories about the good times they had together in Minneapolis, when our two families crammed nine people together in one tiny apartment.

Lyle shares that the night before dad died, they had dinner together and began a game of Rook when dad suddenly sat down on the floor, complaining that he didn't feeling well and needed to go home. The following day, Lyle was horrified to see dad collapse at the pulpit. Lyle never mentions that, instead of immediately taking dad to the nearby Veteran's Hospital, the church men took him to another church—Bethany Chapel, where Prophet David Schoch wasted time praying for him.

Lyle says he'll miss dad every day of his life, then he weeps. Emotions run high as others share stories of dad and how diligent he was in serving the Lord. I watch the adults rejoice—waving and clapping their hands in celebration like clowns at a circus—and I feel the urge to puke. The Pentecostals are giving dad a final send off by saluting Jesus, praising *Him* for accepting Roy into heaven where he'll finally reap the rewards of faithfulness. "That Roy is one lucky holy roller," they think. None of these dummies mention the children—the ones impacted most by his death. My numbed emotions quickly flood back as uncontrollable tears.

Overcome with Jesus fever, the Pentecostals launch into an upbeat hymn, *He The Pearly Gate Will Open*. After the song, Dad's brother Lorelle mans the pulpit to announce through a big smile that *Pearly Gates* was dad's favorite song—one he sang all the time. Lorelle was a soft heart, a much nicer man than Uncle Albin, but his claim that *Pearly Gates* was dad's favorite song perked my skeptical ears. Dad sang only two songs for pleasure: *The Wayward Wind* and *Though God Slay Me Yet I'll Trust Him* which was, as it turned out, a prophetic choice. Dad sang these songs on our never-ending road trips to save the world's sinners—the place where we spent most of our time.

If Lorelle wanted to end the funeral with a snappy tune instead of a bummer, we could have just sung *Pearly Gates* and been done. Instead, he went further by telling his white lie—a Pentecostal half-truth. It was unnecessary, and though I was used to it by now, it still pissed me off. Lying is a *sin*.

Another Viewing

Lyle's wife Eunice escorts me by the hand for a final look at dad's face. It's too much for me—I dig fists into my face and scream. I'm ushered into a private room for prayer. Eunice puts hands on my head and lets her tongue fly, assuming the mindless babbling will calm me, but it only makes me more combative—I've already been through this with her on the day dad died. Trapped and exhausted, I finally relent and let Eunice carry on with her tongue speak, but I've had enough of these morons with their white lies and magic tricks.

The Pentecostal funeral's gleeful praise of Jesus—the celebration of Roy in Heaven —was dishonest. The true celebration for them was in not getting picked—none of them lost a dad or a husband, *thank God*. Their lives hadn't been flipped upside down; In a few hours they'd be right back to normal, eating pie and drinking coffee. Praising Jesus is easy when you aren't the one in the casket.

Dad in casket as I scream off camera

* * *

We pile into the Hearse for the drive out to Harbor Rest, a military cemetery in Costa Mesa twenty-five miles from Long Beach. The driver slowly winds down roads surrounded by orange groves and flatlands as the flowers piled high on dad's casket overwhelm my senses. Squeezed between mom and Albin, and with dad's body behind me, I feel queasy. Gilbert asks the driver how much he makes transporting bodies—he's the man of the house now and knows the future looks bleak.

We arrive at the cemetery and I'm relieved to finally breathe fresh air. The seats are all positioned on one side of the coffin; beyond the coffin sits a big mound of dirt covered with a tarp. Beyond the dirt, a backhoe idles—ready to work.

The Pentecostals arrive and take their seats with us. It's a windy, cold day; light rain forms into beads on the casket. The Pentecostals sing and cry and bark more praise to the Lord for taking dad to Heaven. I'm so tired of their crap—dad's not in Heaven, he's lying right there in the casket.

The time arrives for dad to be lowered into the grave. I peek at the tarp-covered mound of dirt and know what's going to happen. Once we walk away, the backhoe will spring to life, shoveling dirt over dad's coffin and filling his grave. There's no Heaven for dad—just dirt. In a few short minutes, I'll never see him again. My stomach churns and twists.

* * *

Every night of that first week, Gilbert and I joined mom in bed where we all cried together. It was a terrible time—a barren landscape of pain with no comfort in sight. Distant sirens caused me to run wailing into the street. Being with mom helped our broken hearts, but that only lasted a short time until she crashed too. Collapsed.

Mom suffered a complete nervous breakdown that was treated with sedatives and bed rest. As mom receded from view, Gilbert and I were sent to live with Albin & Evelyn. Mark remained in our apartment with mom, and fifteen-year-old Lana disappeared to stay with local cousins. On a visit back to our apartment, I asked to see mom and was pointed to a bedroom door. I peeked inside the room to see her quietly asleep—in the afternoon. It was obvious to the adults that mom couldn't take care of anyone at this point (including herself), but I figured she had abandoned us. Gilbert and I spent a lot of time wondering what the future held.

Albin Rasmussen: The Human Onion

Albin was the sixth son in a farm family of nine siblings. No one knows much about his younger years on the farm besides the fact that his siblings—with the exception of dad—mostly ignored him. Albin was an off-putting man who resembled an onion and wasn't quite right in the head—a doofus with no manners or compassion for others. He was also sneaky like a weasel, behavior even children like us could recognize. Fortunately for Albin, that sneaky nature made him a great salesman to people *stupider than him.* He was God's salesman on earth, a man who spent most of his adult life literally selling the gospel—the floorboard of his car contained bibles and religious pictures he sold door-to-door.

Albin had four children: Joanne, David, Paul, and James. Every morning before school, we all had to get down on our knees and thank Jesus for his daily love and guidance. Only weeks after my dad's *pulpit death*, obnoxious Uncle Albin was forcing me to thank Jesus for being *so good to me.*

"Hey kids, things could be worse," Albin told us, "There's orphans in the world with nobody to care for them. *At least you have me.*" I was very scared at having been abandoned to this man, but I obeyed and did what I was told.

Dad died wearing a cheap watch and holding his weathered bible. One pants pocket contained breath spray (his method of dental hygiene), the other held a five-dollar bill and pocket change. Dad also had the Bel Air, with its trunk packed full of the stuff we acquired on our travels. That was Roy's entire estate—our *Pentecostal inheritance*—but we never received it, because Albin snapped it all up for himself.

As a family always on the move, our belongings were stored in paper bags stuffed inside the car trunk. Bags of clothes, pots & pans, water-damaged bibles, even packs of dad's favorite gum, *Juicy Fruit.* Albin rummaged through all of it, taking what he wanted under the pretense of *storing our belongings.* I watched our former lives disappear into Albin's grabbing hands until nothing remained but plastic flowers and tissues. Whatever Albin didn't want was sold off to any sucker willing to buy it. The man couldn't help himself—it's how he operated his whole life. He even convinced mom that he'd look after dad's Bel Air while she recovered from her nervous breakdown: Once she was back on her feet and stable, he'd return the car. *Never happened.*

I wanted to confront Albin about his pilfering, to ask who gave him permission to steal our stuff from the trunk. Anger sparked inside me and I knew I couldn't be a little girl in this adult world anymore. I had to grow up fast.

The Human Onion & The Prayer Warrior

I asked mom a few years later if she knew that Albin took our belongings. She said she knew but didn't care. I felt so hopeless hearing that.

Three-Hundred-Fifty Pounds of Prayer

Evelyn Rasmussen weighed in the neighborhood of 350 lbs—testament to her terrific cooking skills. In addition to being a good cook, she had breasts like party balloons. Enormous. Dressed in a nightgown while cooking breakfast for us one morning, her left breast fell out. Gilbert and I saw it and our eyes bulged. Evelyn didn't realize it but Albin did, and rather than urge her to cover up he just chuckled. Gilbert and I quickly finished our toast and left the kitchen, spending a lot of time later that day giggling about the Prayer Warrior and her gigantic breast.

Evelyn's cooking was a positive experience for me. Whenever she wasn't on her knees praying, Evelyn was cooking, and her food was filling. In our previous life, dinner was crackers with milk & sugar. With Evelyn it was plates full of meat & potatoes doused with loads of ketchup. Even though this was the woman who uselessly prayed over my dying father—the woman whose enormous butt blocked my view of him—I decided to appreciate my access to regular meals and a warm bed. I overlooked Evelyn's sins.

Light moments aside, the elephant in the room—what happened to dad—always lingered inside Albin & Evelyn's home. I'd go outside to sit and cry alone. I wondered where mom and Mark were, and hoped we wouldn't be forced to live with this sneaky man and his fat wife forever. Life would soon reunify our family, but before that occurred, Gilbert and I were subjected to one final horror—David Rasmussen's movie.

Movie Night with David Rasmussen

Albin's son David—our 16-year-old cousin—was a sickly boy who frequently missed school. As a result, David didn't occupy himself with schoolwork: David's main occupation was entertaining his own thoughts.

One evening while hanging out with me and Gilbert, David told us the story of him taking dad's shoes to school and trying to sell them. "No one wanted the shoes," he laughed. "They were too scuffed and the right one didn't have a lace." David Rasmussen—Albin's son—thought this was funny, and that we'd get a big laugh out of it, too. The tasteless story about dad's unwanted shoes shocked us. I wondered how he got my dad's shoes in the first place, and why he thought to sell them. All signs pointed to Albin, of course.

David topped the evening off by showing us film he shot of dad's funeral. Only weeks after our dad's death, Gilbert and I were now reliving it. Once again we saw dad's face in the open casket. We saw ourselves stood around the casket, crying. My barely formed emotional scab was ripped off by the horrible movie, and I quickly became nauseous. David realized his mistake and shut the film off, but it was too late.

* * *

The Rasmussen adults decided to separate our broken family further. Mom and the boys were sent to Detroit to recuperate over the summer with Bill & Joyce Leigh—old friends from North Central Bible School in Minneapolis. The girls —me and Lana—would remain in Long Beach to finish the last month of school before joining mom in Detroit, or wherever she found herself by then.

I wasn't told of the plan. Mom never said goodbye to me—she just vanished. Gilbert vanished too. Left in the dark, I concluded that mom officially abandoned me to Albin & Evelyn. I was now stuck forever under Albin's thumb, without a brother or mother to defend me; the only real family remaining for me was Lana, a cold-hearted big sister who appeared and disappeared like a phantom. As it turned out, the plane mom boarded with Mark and Gilbert made an emergency landing in an Iowa corn field. They eventually made it to Detroit, but I was oblivious to all of it.

Train Ride Outta Town

Salvation occurred when school ended a few weeks later. Me and Lana were taken to Los Angeles and placed on a train—Destination: Brookings, South Dakota. We were told that dad's brother Herman would meet us at the station, and from there we'd ultimately reunite with mom and our brothers. I was happy to finally leave the custody of Albin & Evelyn, but was nervous to ride alone on a train with Lana.

Lana bit people as a toddler—myself included—and we were all wary of her. As she became older, Lana replaced physical biting with emotional biting; We were wary of that, too. This was the big sister I'd just boarded a train with. It would be a long ride.

IN THE BEGINNING

Elsie Thompson was born at home on May 24, 1922, in the little town of Bruce, South Dakota, to Alfred and Therese Thompson. She had two older siblings: Harold and Thelma. Elsie's mother died when she was two years old and as a little girl she knew nothing about what happened—one day her mom just disappeared. Elsie's sister informed her many years later that her mother suffered a miscarriage at home and bled to death in bed. Elsie's father, a bitter man named Alfred, never uttered a word about it.

After Therese's death, Alfred sent his three children off to different homes: Harold and Thelma went to separate relatives while Elsie went to Alfred's mom. Alfred vowed to never remarry, which wouldn't have been difficult since he was a gross, unlikeable man.

Elsie lived with her grandmother until age nine, when she was returned to Alfred to fend for herself in his cold, empty home. Alfred provided the basics for Elsie—food and a place to sleep—but he never spoke of Therese and barely spoke to her. Elsie watched her dad come and go but he mostly ignored her and left her alone. During cold South Dakota winters, young Elsie covered herself with a horsehair blanket and slept next to the kitchen stove to keep warm. Concerned neighbors kept tabs on Elsie to to make sure she had food and stayed warm—they knew Alfred was a mean, petty man, forever bittered by the loss of his wife and the burden of three kids he didn't like.

Young Elsie also had allies in two local aunts and an uncle: Eva, Sara, and Lee. As Alfred's siblings, they surely knew what kind of man he was and thus took an interest in young Elsie's welfare. Oddly, the three Thompsons were lifelong roommates who never married, but they had warmth in their heart for Elsie, as she did for them. All three were teachers, in contrast to their uneducated brother Alfred who worked at a grain elevator. Alfred's home had a piano—Therese's piano

Elsie Thompson as a baby

—that Elsie learned to play with Aunt Eva's instruction; Little Elsie excelled at it, filling the home with warm chords that echoed inside her lonely heart.

The extended Thompson clan lived in Iowa, so Elsie didn't have much contact with them except for a cousin named Gene—a man she would have married if he wasn't her cousin.

Elsie dearly loved Gene, and her Aunts Eva & Sara and Uncle Lee—honorable family who helped her when she was most in need. That love lasted a lifetime.

Good Life on the Farm

Roy Rasmussen was born October 6, 1922, on Gilbert and Matilda's farm five miles outside of Bruce, South Dakota. When baby Roy arrived in the world, he had five brothers and two sisters; The Rasmussen's first child—a boy named Elmer —died of cancer before Roy was born. As the baby of the family, Roy was spoiled by his mother and siblings, especially sisters Leona and Evelyn. Mother Matilda was grateful for cute little Roy since he was a big improvement over her previous attempt: Albin, a homely baby shaped like an egg.

A curious boy, Roy inadvertently hurt himself while venturing around the family farm. The farmhouse had a potato cellar under the bathroom that was accessed by a trap door in the floor. Left briefly unattended, four-year-old Roy opened the trap door for a peek and fell headfirst into the cellar, landing on a pile of potatoes that rendered him unconscious.

The Rasmussens were tough farmers in tough times. Doctors weren't easily accessible in rural South Dakota, so all the family could do was watch over Roy and hope he woke up. It took two days before he fully regained consciousness.

Many years after dad died, his sister Evelyn Smith visited us in Long Beach. She confessed that she was supposed to watch her little brother on the day he fell into the cellar but lost track of him. Evelyn believed the childhood fall injured his brain, and blamed herself for his untimely death. We assured her that it wasn't her fault—the autopsy determined that he was born with a defect that caused the aneurysm. Evelyn was so happy and relieved; she'd lived with a guilty conscience all those years thinking she caused his death.

The Rasmussens. Front (l-r): Evelyn, Matilda, Gilbert, Leona, Irrin. Rear (l-r): Roy, Albin, Herman, Philip, Lorelle.

Locked Bedroom on the Farm

The Rasmussen farm had a locked bedroom on the second floor that no one was allowed to enter. It was Elmer's room—Gilbert and Matilda's first born—and it's where he stayed while dying of cancer. Elmer knitted in a rocking chair every day until the cancer finally overwhelmed him. The bedroom was now a shrine to Elmer that only Gilbert and Matilda were allowed to see.

As a young girl visiting the farm, I heard the story and twisted it into Elmer's *ghost* occupying the room and staying busy with his rocking-chair knitting. I'd sneak up to the room and give the knob a turn: Yep, it was locked. When our cousins came over, we'd head upstairs for a game of hide-and-seek in the empty rooms (one room had a dusty organ that Matilda used to play at Bruce's Lutheran church). Without fail, we always made sure to visit the room where Elmer's ghost lived. I was the brave one—giving the door a good bang before we all ran off laughing.

The farm house was a fun place for grandkids like myself, with lots of rooms to explore and antiques to rummage through. The same experience would have been had by Roy and his siblings. Dad's warm family life stood in stark contrast to the cold, isolated one lived by mom.

Two Different Families in One Very Small Town

The town of Bruce was (and still is) a one-street town with a population below four-hundred people. Bruce's main street had the necessities: a butcher shop, a Post Office, a bank and a church. Alfred's two-story house was a few yards off main street. A small town like Bruce couldn't have offered much variety from one family to the next, but the Rasmussens—farmers who lived and worked five miles outside of town—were surely different.

Patriarch Gilbert (and his brother Haaken) immigrated from Oslo, Norway. Their birth name *Haugsdal* was changed to *Rasmus,* eventually becoming *Rasmussen.* The family was financially secure and their main asset was being honest, hard-working Norwegians who sealed deals with a handshake.

In contrast to the Rasmussens, the Thompson family history is cloudy since most of them lived in Iowa—away from Alfred. Many of the Thompsons were educated; some were teachers who specialized in education's artistic side. Therese—Alfred's wife, mom's mother—was maiden-named *Ausk,* but nothing more is known of her.

Mom rarely volunteered information on the Thompson family or her father. I asked her about them many times over the years, but after receiving the same

Elsie Thompson Class Photo

downplayed response each time, I eventually gave up. Mom simply didn't want to talk about her early life—the memories were too painful.

Opposites Attract

In Elsie's senior class picture, she's noted as being the class treasurer—a role requiring honesty and smarts. She was pretty and friendly, and her alto/bass-ranged singing voice even earned her spots at town events as part of a popular female trio.

Roy, coming from a hard-working farmer background, had a polite wildness to him —the twinkly-eyed bad boy in today's world. Roy couldn't compete with Elsie's smarts but he was curly-haired handsome and drove a fancy car (courtesy of car-dealing brother Herman) that made everyone in town jealous. It was only a matter of time before these two opposites fell in love.

Alfred Thompson—Elsie's neglectful father—disliked all the farmers living outside of town, considering them low class and disparagingly referring to them as *river rats*. Roy Rasmussen was a river rat and Alfred despised him for it. When Alfred caught wind that Elsie was in love with Roy, he vowed to disown her if they ever married.

Aside from his threat to disown Elsie due to the *river rat* situation, Alfred also squashed her college opportunity, refusing to support a university's offer of a music scholarship for his daughter. For Alfred, women weren't meant to be educated; Considering Therese's death from miscarriage, they were barely meant to have children. Elsie's bitter father wanted nothing for her but servitude—to him.

The only option for Elsie was to get married. She didn't mind that choice, especially since she'd already fallen in love with Roy and the Rasmussens. Despite her dad's threat of disownment, Elsie was ready to marry into Roy's wonderful family. A wedding date was set.

Hateful Sour Widower

Alfred Thompson had a purple mole on his forehead that looked like a grape. From that grape's firm center protruded a single stiff black hair. Alfred—hateful, sour Alfred—wore it with pride.

Alfred thought himself superior to all others in Bruce, a common snob with an overblown ego whose main talent was being vicious to others. After his wife died, he was incapable of loving anyone else—including his three burdensome kids. His vow to never remarry raised no eyebrows because nobody liked him anyways. Alfred hated mankind and mankind hated him back.

After Therese's tragic death, Alfred stored her belongings in a locked trunk kept in the bedroom where she died. Only he knew what the trunk contained. According to mom's sister Thelma, the trunk eventually disappeared and with it all traces of Therese. Whatever love she had for her children was stolen away by a selfish man who wanted it all for himself.

When we were young, mom and dad took us into Bruce to meet Alfred, our *other Grandpa* as mom described him. The attempt was futile. Grandpa Alfred didn't want to meet us, or *her*, or *him*—he literally ran across the street to get away from us, disappearing out of sight. My parents only wanted to share their grandchildren and offer him a nice gift, but Alfred wanted none of it. We were entirely ignored. The gift left at his door was tossed in the trash.

* * *

Elsie & Roy—excited young lovers straight out of high school—looked forward to the future. They were married at the Rasmussen family farm on February 2, 1940. Mom's sister Thelma attended and even sewed mom's dress for her, but brother Harold wasn't there; he likely didn't know about it due to the Thompson siblings' forced estrangement. Alfred was absent—he had no time for *river rats*.

I got to know Thelma many years later and she was a wonderful lady. Thelma talked about her two boys, Gary & Gail, and her husband Bart—who once served time in jail for robbing a bank in Sioux Falls. Thelma was disowned, too.

CHANGING TIMES

Growing up through the 1920s and 30s meant knowing about the Jazz Age and what it represented. For progressive folks, the decadence of it—alcohol, dancing, scantily clad women—was the reason for being. In the Midwest, however, conservative religious families were scared. Very scared. In response to these perceived excesses, Pentecostal Christianity arose, and with it came a laundry list of new rules directed at a single target: Sex.

The Pentecostal movement believed everything promoted by Jazz contributed to premarital sex, and they were probably right. Pentecostal leaders organized summits where like-minded squares strategized a way to combat the Jazz Age's sinful culture. These leaders flexed their muscles, striving to put an end to the reckless jazzers and rescue the unwitting sinners who'd fallen under their spell. The great Pentecostals would lead by example, denying themselves normal desires forever—or at least until their wives complained.

Becoming Pentecostal is easy: a person simply makes a childish verbal promise to *accept Jesus into their heart.* Bonus points accrue for the nutjobs who recruit others into Pentecostalism's isolated society: If you convince a lost soul to make their own accept-Jesus promise—thereby bringing a new Christian into the fold —you'll receive 'witness' credit in Heaven and probably a free pack of gum from the pastor.

The world according to Pentecostals consists of only two types of people: those *with* you and those *against* you. There's no middle ground, and the narrow path of Pentecostalism did (and still does) cause rifts in families who aren't united in religious fervor.

Pentecostalism also promotes the exciting but unsightly practice of *speaking in tongues,* a vocalization similar to the scat-style singing of jazz performers like Ella Fitzgerald and her predecessors. Pentecostals believe speaking in tongues is an on-the-spot takeover of your mouth by the *Holy Spirit*—Jesus in ghost form—resulting in a person babbling out nonsense words to the point of exhaustion, or until another tongue fires up to continue the charade. Call it *good* demon possession.

Through this bizarre practice, the early Pentecostals of the Jazz Age could essentially *scat like Ella* without committing sin. Pastors encouraged their flock to practice this supposed spirit-directed tongue speak in the shower, in their cars—anywhere they could get away with it without being arrested.

Pastor vs Evangelist

Pastors and evangelists occupied different roles in the Pentecostal church of the 1940s:

The pastor operated his church under the rules of Pentecostalism and kept tight control of the congregation's behavior—cracking the whip when necessary to keep the herd in line. Church rules were written and provided in pamphlet form to new converts. The lighter rules regarded media prohibition: No theaters, no television, and no unwholesome radio. Heavier rules existed for the body: No drinking, no dancing, and *definitely* no sex before marriage. Rule-breaking resulted in harsh societal penalties, including public humiliation, expulsion from the church, and blacklisting.

As compensation for their efforts, pastors received pocket-change offerings from their congregation and, more importantly, 10% of the churchgoer's income through a monthly tithe. The tithes are his salary, the offerings are his bonus.

The evangelist's role was traveling from one small town to the next, bringing *foreigner* excitement to isolated people who'd then head to their local church to see what the fuss was about. Charismatic evangelists put on a show with songs, tongue-talking, and the occasional magic trick (like the fake-healing of short legs); By evening's end, a handful of dimwits would line up at the altar, ready to beg admission into *Club Pentecostal* with their very own accept-Jesus promise.

Evangelists collected payment in the form of "special offerings," then they'd load up in the car to do it again in the next town. No salary, just bonuses, but the bonuses could be big—and you'd get them every night you worked.

The pastor / evangelist relationship fed itself: The day-to-day pastor allowed the evangelist to access his people, the fly-by-night evangelist drew new people to the pastor, and round and round it went.

The 1940s Pentecostal movement—especially the evangelists—were a hot ticket in the Midwest. The movement would inevitably land in South Dakota, and when it did, young couples like Roy & Elsie would see a thrilling alternative to a life of farming.

Fire and Brimstone Descend on Bruce

Pentecost landed in Bruce a couple years into Roy & Elsie's marriage when popular evangelist troupe The Horton Sisters showed up for a *tent meeting*—it's exactly how it sounds. Roy & Elsie, unfamiliar but curious about Pentecostalism, attended. The Horton Sister's message of hellfire and brimstone—that unrepentant sinners would be cursed to an eternity of burning—immediately connected with Roy. Made aware of all the terrible sinning occurring outside of Bruce, Roy & Elsie promptly shunned America's popular lifestyle and embraced the strict rules of Pentecostalism. The excitement and energy of Pentecostalism, along with its tall tales—Elsie once reported that prophet Aimee Semple McPherson's words were so powerful that people *held on to light poles to avoid being blown over*—proved a perfect remedy to the Midwest doldrums.

Roy set his sights on becoming an evangelist: the guy who arrived to convert sinners before moving on to the next town. Let the pastor deal with the headaches. Roy and his new wife were already itching to leave the farm and see the world, and now they had a reason—they'd set the world on fire for Jesus.

Standing in challenge to Roy's ambition were two key issues. Evangelists were expected to sing and speak in tongues—indeed, that was their main draw. Though Roy sang well, his voice was thin and harbored an irritating twang. And as a new convert himself, he was still wet behind the ears in the art of tongue speaking. Congregations (and the pastors who owned them) expected an evangelist's set to feature generous helpings of *tongue speak*. Roy needed to master both skills, otherwise he was dead in the water.

Roy was eventually able to lasso his tongue into shape—no easy feat—but try as he might, his voice still retained its tinny twang. Nevertheless, Roy was ordained in the *Firebrands for Jesus* organization and readied himself for life on the road with Elsie second in command. But before he could head full-throttle down the evangelist's road, two babies needed to be born—and a war needed to be fought.

* * *

Roy & Elsie's next couple years were spent car-hopping the Midwest, taking seasonal work and using the downtime in between to build Roy's evangelizing chops. Roy's large family offered a network of relatives and friends who provided rooms for the couple during their travels. Once a year they stayed at a wealthy Christian family's sheep ranch in Hoven, South Dakota, where Roy sheared sheep for a weekly salary. The family loved Roy & Elsie, remarking at how terrific Roy was at shearing their flock.

Though the exciting seed of Pentecost had been planted in them, they hadn't yet perfected the rules and still lived fairly normal Lutheran lives. That normal life occasionally took the couple into nearby Brookings to enjoy sinful movies, and in January 1942 they said hello to their first child: a girl named Lana Deen—named after actress Lana Turner.

Another Brookings child was born the following year on August 22, 1943: Janice Loy—after actress Myrna Loy. The tiny newborn was white-haired and pretty. Tragically, little white-haired Janice never came home—she lived only three days before dying in the hospital. Elsie believed she choked in the nursery while nurses visited with soldiers. An autopsy determined she died of a brain bleed.

Roy still possessed a wooden chest he constructed in school—that chest now became a coffin. Elsie & Roy wrapped baby Janice in a blanket and placed her tiny body in the chest, burying her in an unmarked grave at St. Petri's Lutheran Cemetery near the Rasmussen farm.

At the time, Roy & Elsie lived on the Rasmussen farm with Roy's parents (who'd buried their own son years prior). Gilbert and Matilda Rasmussen—not wealthy but certainly not poor—would surely have purchased a grave marker for their deceased granddaughter. Perhaps they didn't inquire for risk of upsetting the young couple. Perhaps they only knew of the death but not the burial. The details surrounding Janice Loy's unmarked grave can never be answered, but in later years Elsie provided a sad snapshot of herself at the time:

> One rainy night shortly after we buried baby Janice, I stood crying in the farmhouse's kitchen, staring out the window as a thunderstorm flooded the distant landscape. I thought about my little white-haired baby lying in that chest, buried under the dirt—now mud—knowing she was cold and alone. I wanted to hold my baby, to keep her warm in the rain, but I couldn't. I was powerless to comfort my little daughter.

Mom rarely spoke about the past—preferring to keep bad memories locked away from the present—but she disclosed Janice Loy's fate and her unmarked grave. Mom never mentioned dad grieving. She never mentioned dad comforting her. That's because Roy Rasmussen was a spoiled momma's boy: he had no compassion for anyone but himself.

The Horton Sisters arrive in Bruce

These ladies brought a revival to Bruce, South Dakota in the early 1930's. As a result, George and Stella Sterud and other relatives found Christ, thus beginning the faith that would endure for generations to come.

Rear of Horton Sisters photo

WORLD WAR TWO:
A PENTECOSTAL'S TOUR

In early 1944, the young Rasmussens found themselves living with cousins Lyle & Eunice Lenning in Long Beach, California. Albin was also in Long Beach, and since Roy had a habit of following in his brother's footsteps, it's a fair guess that he followed Albin to Long Beach for a job opportunity or an evangelizing mission —perhaps both. Roy was also a student at the California Aircraft Institute in Los Angeles; That's where he was when Uncle Sam came calling, drafting Roy into the Army on March 13th. The military wanted Lyle and took him, too.

Roy & Lyle completed their medical clearances at Fort MacArthur in San Pedro, California, before being bussed out to boot camp in Abilene, Texas. After basic training, Lyle was split off from Roy to learn aircraft gunnery, eventually breaking his eardrum and receiving a medical discharge. Roy wasn't slated for flight: his boots remained firmly on the ground in Denver, where he trained as a medic.

The role of a medic in wartime—providing frontline aid to wounded soldiers—is extremely dangerous, because the enemy already knows where to find you. For a man more interested in saving souls than saving bodies, this job assignment would prove a big problem for Pentecostalism's newest draftee.

The military provided bus transport for wives to follow their husbands, and Elsie rode those buses with little Lana at her side. Unfortunately, the buses were also filled with drunken soldiers—some going to war, others returning from it. Elsie later bragged that she worked hard during those bus trips to keep two-year old Lana seated on her lap without making a fuss. When asked how she kept safe from the out-of-control soldiers, Elsie's reply was simple: Jesus protected them.

During medic training in Denver, the dormant seed of Pentecost—planted in Roy two years earlier by The Horton Sisters—finally sprouted. Private Rasmussen became a major problem in the barracks, aggressively pushing the gospel on recruits who wanted nothing of his harassment. Pacing the halls while crying out to Jesus from the top of his tinny voice, Roy induced more fear in young recruits than Nazi Germany. Something had to be done about it.

For young men soon to be fighting a war, death was top of mind. The same could be said for 22-year-old husband and father Roy Rasmussen. Though Roy's behavior was intended to save *other* men's souls before they went off to die, he certainly considered his own as well. "Where can I better serve the Lord?" Roy thought. "At home with my wife and child? Or in Europe—where my shrill voice will be drowned out by the screams of dying men?"

For two loud months, Private Rasmussen pressed on with his barracks evangelism, exhorting fellow recruits to take action *while they still can.* He sang songs and cried out to the Lord—just like he saw The Horton Sisters do. Roy bleated out to the barracks, "Jesus! Save these men! Save them before it's too late—*ah-sha-lahdabahma-ding-dong!*"

The other men—minds fixed on the violent future awaiting them—shunned Roy. "When the Germans wound us on the battlefield," they wondered, "Will Private Rasmussen still be shouting for Jesus?"

On July 15, 1944—before deploying to Europe—the Army decided they'd had enough. Private Roy Rasmussen was discharged for being mentally unfit. His soul was saved.

* * *

Though he'd served only four months before discharge, the military was good to Roy. They paid a survivor's benefit to Elsie and her children until age 18—benefits that proved crucial to the family's survival in tough times. Roy, of course, didn't know any of that in July 1944. In fact, the only thing on Roy's mind in the summer of '44 was having *another Janice.*

Conceived in August 1944, the *second* Janice Loy (that's me) was born nine months later in Hoven, South Dakota—the same town where Roy sheared sheep. Roy returned to familiar territory after his military discharge, taking seasonal work and supplementing his income with sales of bibles and religious pictures. It wasn't much to live on for the young Pentecostals, but Roy & Elsie knew in their hearts that Jesus would provide for them; On those occasions when he *didn't,* they could always fall back on Gilbert & Matilda Rasmussen—parents who couldn't say no to their baby boy.

Roy thumped his bible in the barracks. The Army thumped him out.

Sioux Falls

Roy considered his future while bouncing between seasonal work and the family farm, ultimately deciding to move up to Sioux Falls, South Dakota, about an hour away from Bruce. An old bank building there had recently been converted into affordable apartments, offering Roy an exciting opportunity at city life with his family. He secured one, and the young couple (with three-year-old Lana and months-old Janice) moved into their new home.

The apartment had cement floors and a big kitchen sink that made a perfect bathtub for squirming babies like myself. Mom recalled how cute dad looked while bathing me. Unfortunately, during one bath he lost his grip on my soapy body and dropped me to the floor. Dad urgently called to mom for help as I lay on the floor screaming; Mom came to the rescue, picking me up and confirming that I was fine. Dad's crying ceased, replaced with pride that I survived the fall.

Assemblies of God

Roy attained relative stability for his family in Sioux Falls. His Pentecostal ambition to save souls persisted though, so he and Elsie continued honing their evangelical skills at any church that would accept them.

Their efforts were rewarded sometime in 1946 when they became affiliated with the *Assemblies of God* organization, a fast-growing Pentecostal franchiser. The Assemblies were looking for savvy young couples to spread their message far and wide;

Instead, they found Roy & Elsie—simple, pliable people from a farming town of 300.

To be fair, they had talent: dad strummed guitar, mom played accordion, and together they sang duets. Dad could also whip himself into a legitimate tongue-talking frenzy, something I'd witnessed as a young girl through his morning prayer routine: dad on his knees with head tilted skyward, hands clapping high above his head as tongue gibberish flowed from his mouth. I always thought he was being funny or playing a game with me, but I couldn't be more wrong—Roy's selfish relationship with Jesus could never allow time for his daughter.

Most importantly for the Assemblies, Roy & Elsie were willing to go the extra mile for them—literally. The Assemblies needed evangelists to work California's Central Valley: A rural, sweaty swathe of distantly connected agricultural towns occupied by uneducated poor people—people like us. The Assemblies' mission would require lots of driving, but long drives didn't bother Roy & Elsie since brother Herman owned a car dealership that provided replacement wheels anytime Roy needed them. That's not to suggest Herman or the rest of the Rasmussens were thrilled by Roy's (and Albin's) choice of religion: As Lutherans, they saw the new-fangled Pentecostals as kooky people behaving oddly. But Roy—baby Roy—would always find support from family.

In accepting the AoG's mission, Roy ignored the fatherly responsibility he had to two young children and a third on the way. The Assemblies provided no provisions for lodging, plus he had to send them 10% of what he earned as a tithe. And Roy's only contacts in the Central Valley were brother Albin (who preceded him to Stockton with Evelyn) and their ring-leading cousin Fred Lenning. Roy & Elsie would now go forth and test their faith, as well as the patience of pastors and acquaintances they leaned on along the way. One pregnant wife, two tiny children, and a man aflame for the Lord crammed into a Chevy to bring the Gospel to California's dusty-eyed farmers. God would provide.

WELCOME TO THE CENTRAL VALLEY

The Rasmussens proved a moderate hit with the tiny churches dotting the Central Valley. Elsie played her accordion in time with Roy's plucked guitar and their voices—her alto/bass, his soprano—combined in a catchy Midwestern twang that the Okies loved. They were cute despite Roy's distracting eye blink, and though he tried firing them up with sermons, the real draw was always their songs.

Once the offerings were counted and 10% set aside for the AoG, Roy & Elsie would bed down for the night wherever they could, be it church housing or the car. Meals were a minor concern—especially for the kids. In the rural Central Valley, it wasn't unusual for us to sleep in the car on empty stomachs. All came second to God.

In the days following a big Sunday sermon, Roy would learn his next destination by phoning cousin Fred Lenning, a snake-eyed man who knew all the churches in the Central Valley network.

Fred Lenning was an extremely dodgy Pentecostal fixer who forever reeked of body odor and liquor. Fred made no secret of disliking all of his ten children, and he urged Roy, Albin, and Lyle to enforce obedience in their wives through regular spankings. Fred's primary role in the church network was to *enrich himself through it,* a task he accomplished through management of Roy, Albin, and Lyle—men he held great sway over.

Fred claimed to have raised a young boy from the dead in the basement of a house in Brookings, South Dakota. Roy & Elsie were there praying over the boy; they saw him rise with their own eyes. Years later it was explained that the boy wasn't dead: he was merely unconscious after hitting his head. These types of white-lie stories were wildly popular in Pentecostal circles, used to burnish the credentials of lying opportunists and self-appointed prophets—men like Fred Lenning—who were happy to dupe hayseeds into forking over their paychecks for the Christian *magic show.* Roy, Albin, and Lyle, hayseeds themselves, also told those lies—they just happened to believe them.

Once Fred directed dad's next move, we'd load up in the car and head off to no-man's land. Mom kept Lana and me at bay as dad—map in hand—drove down yet another rural road. For hunger we had crackers. For potty breaks we had the rear tire or the ditch beyond. For the heat we had windows, and for entertainment we had dad practicing scales with mom joining in.

Church offerings are spotty at best, and people attending the small churches visited by Roy & Elsie had tight pockets. Roy's family in South Dakota wired money as needed to support him, but they had no clue that we lived in a car much of the time, or that his children often went hungry. The Assemblies were no help at all since money went only one way for them—from Roy's hand to theirs. But, blinded by Pentecost, Roy & Elsie pressed on.

Mom enjoyed telling the story of when our family lived in a *chicken coop* for a few months during the Central Valley excursion. A pastor in their network lived on a farm in the city of Turlock and hosted visiting preachers inside his converted chicken coop. Mom bragged how cute it was, how she used her sewing machine (kept in our car trunk) to stitch my clothes into a curtain that shaded the coop's make-shift window. She considered those times with Roy to be the *good old days;* It never occurred to her that we were homeless by choice, routinely living off the goodwill of others, and—at that moment in time—residing in a chicken coop. Her fond reminiscence of Roy always ignored the children who suffered.

* * *

After many months on the road between Bakersfield, Visalia, Fresno, and beyond, Elsie told Roy she needed a break to birth her next child. Albin was nearby, having lived in Stockton for the past year running a fledgling church with Evelyn, who was popular with the locals. With the family connection (and anticipated helping hands), Roy decided that Stockton was the best place for temporary settlement, and that's where Gilbert was born in March 1947.

Albin & Evelyn must have noticed how pathetic we were. Mom spoke proudly in later years of our itinerant lifestyle; Of how we moved ten times in thirteen months, earning little money as she and dad evangelized up and down the Central Valley. The impact of that constant instability showed on our family: This was, after all, when Lana first started biting people—including me. Perhaps Lana wanted attention from parents only interested in themselves.

Dad & mom were acquainted with the King family, friends of Fred Lenning who lived in Clovis and offered us a room at their home anytime we were in the area.

Me and Gilbert in Stockton, California.

Once Gilbert was sturdy enough to travel, we found our way back to Clovis to take the Kings up on their offer.

During our time with the Kings, I made my own move for attention. One method was by faking convulsions at the dinner table: I'd roll my eyes up into my head and shake my body to cause panic among everyone in the room—everyone but mom, who knew the routine and scolded me for my behavior.

The King Family made an odd request at this time that illuminates just how poor we looked—they asked to adopt me. Rather than horrified, mom was honored that an established Christian family like the Kings wanted to adopt her white-haired drama queen. Mom couldn't see how neglected her children actually were: we slept in cars and chicken coops and strangers' homes, and we barely ate—all for dad's self-serving quest to save the souls of *other* people. Mom politely declined the King's offer, although dad kept quiet—did he really need that extra daughter?

I had one more chance at drama before we left the Central Valley for good. During a church service in Clovis, mom & dad sang from the stage while I sat in the pews with dusty farmer kids who *oohed* and *ahhed* at me: the blue-eyed three-year-old from South Dakota. Happy to be away from mom's disciplinary hand, I stood up in the middle of their song and mischievously yelled, "Ha ha mommy, you can't get me now!" The congregation erupted with laughter and praised Jesus for sending such a funny little angel into their midst. And I got the attention I craved.

HOMEWARD BOUND

Roy & Elsie's soul-saving expedition to the Central Valley wrapped up after a year or two, and in 1949 the family found itself back in Bruce to nurse its wounds. Out of money and with Lana age seven, myself age four, and Gilbert still only two years old, it was time for Roy to chart a more stable course for himself—within the world of Pentecostalism, of course.

While considering next moves, dad & mom refreshed their car at brother Herman's car dealership in nearby De Smet, South Dakota. In the meantime, the rest of us fell into great luck—we got to stay at our grandparent's farm.

The Farm

Grandpa & Grandma's farm gave us a break from the turmoil of dad & mom's religious mania. We visited many times over the years, and it was always exciting to round the corner of a little dirt road outside of Bruce and suddenly see Grandpa's big red barn in the distance. Serenity washed over me and I couldn't wait to get in there for warm hugs and coffee with my Grandma.

Cousins were always around the farm, so we'd get together in Grandpa's barn to play the simple games kids played, hiding behind big bales of hay and chasing each other round-and-round. Children's games are easy and carefree, filling young hearts with innocent laughter and companionship. Our life on the road was any-thing but that: Empty stomachs, lonely drives, and church weirdos wagging their tongues. Dad's angry sermons were hell, but the farm games were heaven.

Far off on the other side of the corn fields was another farm where Grandpa's brother Haaken lived with his wife Esther and two daughters, Darlene and Mavis. Lana chose to stay there, preferring to separate herself from immediate family as much as possible. Separating the two farms was a river; Lana spent much time walking along that river, lost in thought. When Lana's river froze over in the winter, I attempted to skate it. I failed.

Grandpa & Grandma Rasmussen. Grandma only spoke Norwegian.

Grandma Matilda

My first coffee experience occurred at the farm. Each morning I'd sit at the kitchen table next to a big black stove (kindled with wood and corn cobs) and watch Grandma slice off a big slice of homemade bread. She'd load it with butter and maple syrup, then give me a cream-and-sugared coffee to wash it down. It was divine. Grandma was so sweet and I remember feeling how perfect she was—I never wanted to leave her side.

I chased kittens and baby chickens on the farm, and happily helped Grandma gather eggs from the grouchy hens who didn't want them taken. We laughed together when the chickens cackled and scolded us for snatching their eggs. Grandma Matilda was fun and had a great sense of humor; I can see why dad loved her so much.

Lutherans Pass on Pentecost

Gilbert & Matilda Rasmussen—immigrants from Norway—were Lutherans who didn't embrace Pentecostalism, not even a little. Roy and Albin were the only siblings who pursued it full throttle; brothers Irrin and Lorelle attended a Pentecostal church but went no further with it. Being around nice people like my grandparents illustrated how pleasant dad & mom's future could have been had they not fallen for a cult which taught that all other Christians were going to hell. Pentecostalism turned ignorant people into angry, self-righteous assholes, perpetually promising that the great apocalyptic *rapture* would end the world in ten years—and perpetually failing to see their own promise realized.

With a head full of apocalypse, Roy most certainly suggested to family that they turn from their wicked ways before it was too late. Surely that advice was based in love for them, but it was also the epitome of Pentecostal arrogance. Grandpa Rasmussen, on the other hand, avoided extremes and instead saw the practicality of things. I once overheard Grandpa suggest to dad that he settle down and take care of his family. To a crazy Pentecostal like dad, that advice fell on deaf ears. Roy just needed money and a car from his brother Herman—he knew better than his father because Pentecostals always knew better than everyone else.

Grandpa & Grandma's efforts eventually paid off though. In 1949, Roy decided to move his family-of-five to Minneapolis and attend North Central Bible Institute. Minneapolis was only a few hours from Bruce—light years closer than California —so Roy would retain easy access to family handouts while also further feeding his religious appetite. As an added benefit, Roy's cousin Lyle Lenning (and wife Eunice) already lived there—we'd have a place to stay.

TOUCHED BY A PROPHET

Since North Central Bible Institute wasn't free and neither family had much money, the Lennings shared their apartment with us when we first arrived. Roy and Lyle weren't the single-and-ready-to-mingle college kids of today, they were family men with young children—Roy had three, Lyle had two. With a grand total of *nine* humans, the upstairs two-bedroom apartment was far too small. All the kids shared a single bedroom, and in that bedroom they shared a single bed: Me & Gilbert plus cousins Ronnie & Jerry; Lana was there as well—she couldn't have been anywhere else—but she was too cultured for our cousin soup and slept in the closet. The adults shared the other bedroom: Lyle & Eunice in one bed, Roy & Elsie in another. A blanket hung from the ceiling to divide the room between Rasmussens and Lennings—presumably so husbands wouldn't get confused in the dark and crawl into the wrong bed. With blankets, pajamas, and people everywhere, the Lenning apartment was one giant slumber party.

Lyle & Eunice Lenning: Good People

Lyle & Eunice were true friends who always looked out for mom. Lyle was a mild man whose twangy Midwestern voice barely rose above a whisper, and though he was firmly committed to the message of Pentecost, he was never offensive or in-your-face about it. In contrast to his scoundrel brother Fred—who raised living men from the dead and called it a miracle—Lyle was an honest man who saw no opportunity in lies.

Lyle was never successful in the ministry and Eunice eventually pulled the plug on his aspirations, convincing him to take the common-sense path of real employment: a Post Office job in Long Beach. It was there—when we were most in need—that Lyle shined.

Eunice also kept a watchful eye over us, and she remained a friend-to-the-end with mom. Decades later, I listened to them both laugh about the Army buses they rode

Lyle & Eunice Lenning were always good to us

to follow their recruited husbands around. I liked Eunice and realized she cared about me—she knew I was an innocent little girl thrust into a terrible situation. As a mother without a daughter, Eunice saw herself in me and thus gave me more focus than I preferred. The day dad died—when Eunice pissed me off with her tongue-talking prayers at my moment of greatest distress—she comforted me in the only way she knew how. Eunice did her best for me.

North Central Bible School

Dad eventually moved us into a North Central dorm apartment designated for married couples with children. It consisted of a small bedroom and bathroom, and a tiny kitchenette. After having lived in a car for much of the Central Valley, the cramped apartment didn't really bother us.

For income, dad parked cars part-time at a local garage in Minneapolis. Seven-year-old Lana even contributed money by ironing shirts for students (standing on a stool to reach the ironing board). Dad and mom didn't look my way for a contribution, but I was aware of the money situation and decided to cut my dinner portions in half—instead of twenty peas, I ate only ten.

North Central Bible Institute was run by the Assemblies of God, the same Pentecostal organization that sent Roy & Elsie evangelizing throughout California's

North Central Bible Institute with dad & mom. Front (l-r): Gilbert, me, Lana.

Central Valley. Their hard work and popularity surely raised their status within the AoG; attending the AoG's college strengthened that relationship.

Roy was well liked at North Central and he was elected President of both the Junior and Senior Classes. He also served as student chairman of the school's advertising department—the yearbook pictured him seated at a desk surrounded by other students. Even though Elsie was a non-student whose time was spent tending to her children, she also made an appearance in the yearbook—seated at a banquet table as Roy speaks into a microphone.

Roy & Elsie—two attractive, talented Pentecostals—were up-and-coming stars for the movement. With graduation soon approaching, the Assemblies of God conceived a new mission for Roy & Elsie Rasmussen. But first, a prophecy needed to be heard.

False Prophet

David Schoch was a big deal with Pentecostals and himself. The *little angry prophet from Pas-a-de-na* operated under the Latter Rain branch of Pentecostalism which fashioned itself as more extreme than AoG, but these branches were all just variations on the same flavor and their church networks duly overlapped.

In 1952, Prophet Schoch and other big shots were scheduled to appear at a camp meeting in Spearfish, South Dakota—just a short drive out from Minneapolis. Camp meetings were large tented events attended by thousands of Pentecostals desperate for excitement since virtually everything was off-limits to them. At camp meetings, they could finally sing, shake, and engage in Pentecostal-approved wackiness, and they'd do it with a thousand other weirdos from across the region. Besides entertaining the common folk, camp meetings also offered networking opportunities for the players—those people who knew what was *really* going on. Self-appointed prophet David Schoch was a player. His prophecies—God's words spoken by man—were universally respected, and AoG leaders could put those words to good use in building their next generation of ministers.

The upcoming camp meeting was major news at the Assemblies' North Central Bible Institute—a college built to groom ministers—and would serve as a launching pad for rising stars of the Assemblies of God brand. Roy & Elsie—those rising stars—dutifully loaded up the family and headed out to Spearfish to attend.

At the camp meeting, a luncheon occurred before the big evening service, with David Schoch and other high-profile ministers meeting-and-greeting the invitees. Class President Roy Rasmussen and wife Elsie were invited, and it was there that they first met the mighty David Schoch. According to Elsie, David Schoch praised their work in the Central Valley and inquired of their future ministerial plans. Time was short with the Prophet though—other up-and-comers were waiting in the wings to offer him a clammy handshake—so Roy & Elsie returned to their seats, thrilled at having met a living prophet. An *actual* living prophet.

Returning that evening with their children, Roy & Elsie marveled at the unforgettable sight of the Spearfish camp meeting: A single mass of sweaty Pentecostals

—a thousand or more—all hopping up and down as worship leaders led them in childish singalongs. At song conclusions—when emotional praise chords were sustained for ten minutes or more—a thousand tongues flapped wildly in dry mouths. The power—the stench—of the Lord caused fainting spells throughout the mass. A fresh low-energy song would begin, offering a moment of respite for the frenzied mass. Recuperation. Water. Breath mints.

Then the Prophet rolled in.

I was there, age seven. Gilbert and Lana were there, too. Prophet David Schoch, all sixty-six inches of him, thundered into his sermon. I heard it—we all heard it —but the frenzied Christian mass was impatient. Agitated. They knew what they wanted. Get to the prophecies, David, that's what we're here for—*it's why God put you on this earth.*

"Roy Rasmussen!"

Roy's eyes go wide. His blinker eye twitches, then holds fast.

"God calls you to the stage, Roy Rasmussen."

Elsie remains with her children as Roy makes the walk. The sweaty mass of Christians crack open for him like the Red Sea. Reaching the stage, Roy's scalp is touched by a gentle hand—the hand of a prophet.

"Roy Rasmussen, you are a servant of the Lord."

Roy's well-versed in the protocol of prophecy. He closes his eyes.

"You will do many great things in the name of Christ, Roy Rasmussen. Do you see it, Roy? Lands across this great country and lands unseen by man. Do you see it, Roy?"

Roy's mind conjures an image of a map. A globe. The Heavens. Protocol directs his next move—it's time to mouth off.

"Ah-sha-lahdabahma-ding-dong!"

A thousand excited tongues flap inside the sweaty Christian mass. The tent's trapped humidity fogs the air. A light rain falls.

"Far and wide you will travel, Roy Rasmussen, bringing truth to lost souls around the world!

Roy's tongue flies on autopilot, *"Ah-sha-lahma-ding-dong, bada-bing-bong-bada-boom!"*

"Go forth, Roy, to the North and South! The East and West call you, Roy Rasmussen. Go there!"

Roy knows what comes next. Protocol.

"Jesus commands—You obey. Down, Roy!"

Roy falls backward, landing on the sawdust floor with a dusty thud. Ministers descend on Roy as he convulses in a fit of tongues. I thought he died.

My child's intuition was more accurate than I thought: Dad's death would indeed come after being touched by David Schoch, but five years later at Schoch's Bethany Chapel. The prophecy was false.

* * *

Roy Rasmussen—North Central's now-blessed star—graduated in 1952 from the Bible Institute and was quickly chartered by the Assemblies of God to build a church in Chisago City, an annoyingly named small town forty miles from Minneapolis. It was a church-building mission in the most literal sense: Roy would supervise construction of a Quonset hut church from the ground up. The Assemblies financed the project and would provide Roy with a small stipend until buildout was complete, whereupon Roy would then serve as minister of the new church. The Assemblies even devoted ad space in North Central's yearbook for the mission, picturing Roy at the empty build site and urging students to join him and other Christians as they sawed and hammered their way to salvation.

Before any of that could happen though, Roy needed to find a home for his family. His search took us to a cabin in the woods.

Monster Bugs at a Lakeside Cabin

The dingy, tired forest cabin near the lake could have been beautiful with caring owners. For us—poor wanderers living hand-to-mouth—it was an ugly place that we'd soon make worse. An insect screen wrapped around the entire cabin to protect occupants from monstrous lake bugs waiting to feast on humans. Unsurprisingly, that screen had already been breached, so we were on the defensive the moment we moved in. The kitchen was dimly lit, with cupboards set too high for a normal person to reach, so mom placed a stool between the sink and fridge so dad could access the dishes without resorting to acrobatics. Lana, Gilbert, and I shared a dank bedroom while mom & dad slept privately in another. In their room, future brother Mark was conceived.

The cabin had an outdoor enclosure that mom & dad filled with chickens to raise for eggs and food. I loved animals and frequently went outside to play with the chickens, singling one out as a favorite: my little friend *Cock-a-Doodle-Doo*.

Since Albin & Evelyn were also floating around the area, they sent their older daughter Joann to live with us; Joann pitched-in money from her job at the town grocery to help with expenses. While dad awaited approval to break ground on the church, he took a job at the local *Montgomery Wards* department store to supplement his meager AoG stipend.

Gilbert Acts Up

After a few months in neutral, the church plan was finally approved and work began. Dad quit his department store job to manage the construction effort, which wasn't too complicated since it was a single-level Quonset Hut with only a few doors and windows. Most of the labor came from volunteer North Central students and alumni who wanted to join other Christians in partaking of the *fruits of the spirit* while earning brownie points from higher-ups in the Pentecostal network.

It was in our cabin that young Gilbert acted out for the first time, climbing atop the kitchen stool and spitting on Lana's head as she walked past. Lana ran to mom, who promptly shoved a bar of soap into Gilbert's mouth and made him eat it. Fire-and-brimstone Christians adhered to the *spare the rod, spoil the child* teaching popularized by preachers of the time—indeed it was one of mom's favorite bible verses—and the stress of the time put our parents on hair triggers. Dad's weapon of choice wasn't a soap bar but a swinging belt; he lit up at every opportunity to slide leather from his pant loops and wield it against us.

A Murder in Town

Money was tight (as it always was) and chicken eggs weren't enough for us to eat, so one afternoon mom decided she'd catch and cook a chicken— that chicken happened to be my little friend *Cock-a- Doodle-Doo*. She chased him down in the pen, capturing the frightened bird and swinging him by the neck in tight circles while I listened to him squawk. Mom was proud of catching him—even prouder that she killed him—and fried the bird up for dinner that night. I was deeply upset with her and refused to eat, and for the next few weeks I avoided interacting with her; I truly disliked her for murdering my little friend. She could have chosen any other chicken—why mine?

* * *

Having completed church construction, and with pregnant mom growing in size, dad found a better living arrangement for us: a respectable two-story house on an actual street. Perhaps finances improved—the Assemblies may have paid Roy a bonus for completing the church—or maybe he felt it would look better if the new church's pastor didn't *live in the woods*. Regardless, it was a move towards normalcy and a nice change for us.

In small Chisago City—population below 800—a new church built from the ground up would have been big news. Roy's hot prospect was a dud, however —the only attendees were North Central students and alumni who helped build the church, or curious North Central-affiliated people who wanted to see it for themselves. Pentecostal Christianity is like an anchovy—you either love it or you don't—and the natives of Chisago City took a hard pass on the wacky new religion arriving in their town.

Church failure aside, dad could still be proud of his successful project management. He also showed the ability to work a regular job at *Montgomery Wards*. We were in a nice house now and I got to attend a real school with classmates and structure. We even had friendly neighbors who invited us kids over on Monday nights to watch *I Love Lucy* while mom & dad spent time alone. Baby Mark was soon born in neighboring St Croix, Wisconsin, and brought back to our budding home life in Chisago City. Things were looking up for our family in 1953, but I knew this normal life would have to end. It always did.

Roy's Belt Loosens

I was tasked to watch over baby Mark one day while my parents ran errands. Annoyed that Lana wasn't asked instead, I sat there watching Mark sleep until boredom set in and I went outside to play. That was a huge mistake—dad and mom came home shortly thereafter and caught me outside. Enraged, dad took me to an upstairs bedroom and forced me to lay across the bed. I shook with fright as he slid out his belt; I cried when he whipped me with it. Even though I was fond of him in a basic *dad* sense, Roy never formed a relationship with me— he didn't even try. Now this man who barely knew me was whipping me with a belt, causing me physical and emotional pain. I was confused—crushed—by his actions, and from that moment on I viewed him very differently.

* * *

Dad parted ways with the Assemblies of God after the church failure—or maybe they parted ways with him. Regardless, he hitched his wagon to the Latter Rain

The Quonset Hut church that dad built for Assemblies of God.

branch of Pentecostalism—the same branch that Prophet David Schoch belonged to. The Latter Rain were at the forefront of Pentecostal extremism and perhaps dad saw a brighter future there than the slower-moving Assemblies of God.

Meanwhile, Albin and Fred Lenning were in his ear. "It's time to move," they said. "Go back to Bruce and reload, then get your ass back out on the road—those sinners can't save themselves."

Mom begged dad to stay in Chisago City, to buy our two-story rental with his GI Bill and put down roots. The townspeople were nice, the city was young, and the house was a perfect fit for our family of six. Dad refused. He needed to save souls, and Chisago City was already dead.

Chisago City lasted about a year. I attended first grade for some of that time and almost made it through the school year before we abruptly left. Gone—just like that. Years later I asked mom what happened to our stuff at the house and she claimed a poor memory. "We probably gave it to a family who needed it more than we did," she suggested. A white lie, of course—nobody could have needed it more than us.

Staged photo of Pastor Roy & Elsie in the new church.

Another staged photo featuring North Central students.

Bible Study in Chisago City. In front are Lana, me, and Gilbert.

Our nice home in Chisago City. Mom begged dad to stay.

SPINNING WHEELS

Roy & Elsie left Chisago City (and the Assemblies' new church) for the home-town comfort of Bruce, South Dakota, except this time their family was too large to stay at the Rasmussen farm. The couple—both just into their thirties—now carted around the near teen-aged Lana, me, Gilbert, and barely-a-toddler Mark. Still devoted to his Pentecostal mission, and still without real work, Roy needed somewhere to stay—preferably rent free—while the Lord drew up a new destina-tion for him. Grandpa & Grandma, as always, came through for their little boy by negotiating a deal with the Skovlunds, cousins who owned a farm across the road from the Rasmussens.

<u>The Skovlund Family</u>

Grandpa Gilbert and Ludwig Skovlund were distant cousins by marriage, but in the Norwegian farms in and around Bruce, pretty much everyone was a cousin. Gilbert was the biggest name around the farms, a trusted man who built up decades of good will through his generosity and wisdom. Considering the Skovlund's opin-ion of Roy, he'd need all the good will he could get.

Ludwig and the other Skovlund men knew *all about* Roy Rasmussen. He was a slacker, the little boy who kept coming home to beg mama for money. They knew about his tongue twirlin' religion, and the fancy cars Herman gave him so he could drive his poor family into the ground. Most of all, they knew about his time in the army—when he faked insanity to get kicked out before having to go off and fight. The Skovlunds had a boy drafted, too—he died fighting in Europe. Roy Rasmussen ducked the war, and the Skovlund men didn't like him for it. Not one bit.

The broader Rasmussen and Skovlund families got along—it was only Roy they disliked. But of the two families, Grandpa Gilbert held the most sway, and he eventually worked out a deal with Ludwig (and son Wendall) that allowed Roy to live in Wendall's vacant farmhouse for free.

Farmhouse of Horrors

Dad celebrated this victory; Once again, Jesus delivered when Roy needed him most. We headed to our new home to meet its owner, Wendall.

The first thing I noticed about Wendall Skovlund—the only thing—was his missing right arm. Mom said he lost it in a corn picker: a scary industrial machine used by farmers to make hard jobs simple. In a corn picker, the cobs occasionally get stuck in the rollers, jamming the machine and requiring the farmer to reach in and remove it. Wendall reached in one day and the rollers grabbed his arm, snapping it off at the elbow and sending it down the chute with the corn cobs. This was the man who owned the farmhouse—the man allowing war-dodger Roy Rasmussen to squat rent-free for the next few months. Sort of a landlord. Sorta not.

The farmhouse had no keys because the farmhouse had no locks. There was no modern plumbing—water was pumped by hand in the kitchen, always coming out black until you pumped it clear. Our toilet was an outhouse with a fancy two-seater bench and smoothed corn cobs for wiping. Bathing was performed in the kitchen, inside a large tub next to the stove (to keep the water hot). Since pumping water into the tub was so difficult, we shared the same bath water. It was a terrible place for anyone to live, let alone a family of six.

Door-to-Door Sales

While we fended for ourselves at the horrible farmhouse, dad traveled to nearby Brookings to sell Fuller Brush makeup kits and his always-stocked religious paraphernalia. Door-to-door sales were always dad's fallback, and given the wide variety of merchandise he carried in his satchel, he was probably difficult to get rid of once he appeared at your front door:

> "Can I interest you in a makeup kit, ma'am? No? Okay—how about this stunning illustration of our baby Lord Jesus in a manger? No? Okay—do you like *chewing gum*, ma'am?"

Homeowners probably bought something just so they could resume whatever they were doing before he knocked.

Dad's good salesmanship wasn't just down to persistence, mom also lent a hand with her sewing skill. Our car trunk always carried a sewing machine, and besides sewing curtains for chicken coops, mom also touched-up dad's tattered clothes.

However, some clothing items—like the floppy cuffs of dad's shirt sleeves—were beyond repair and needed a more *mechanical* touch. Dad had worn his shirts for so long that the forearms & elbows had gaping tears where the fabric finally gave up, causing the cuffs to pull out too far when he wore a jacket. Mom's novel fix was to pin the sleeve portions together, then snap a *rubberband* around the sleeve to dad's arm. Pulling a jacket over this contraption allowed the shirt cuffs to stay at the correct length, and nobody would ever know what lurked underneath Roy's coat. You'd only know something was amiss if his hands turned blue.

Dad's rubber-bands-and-safety-pins suit eventually helped him move up to a job selling vacuums at Sears, a regular drop of income to supplement the irregular drips that kept us barely alive.

Sears Catalog

Farmers in the area stocked their outhouses with de-kerneled corn cobs for wiping; A perk of dad's Sears gig was our unlimited supply of glossy catalog pages to use instead of those cobs. My first memory of doing anything fun with Lana was when we sat in our two-seater outhouse—the wooden plank with two holes cut in it. We ripped out Sears catalog pages, folding the thick paper carefully to eliminate any sharp edges. Once we had our sheets ready, we held singing contests and judged each other's performance. Lana always won, of course.

Lana's favorite outhouse song was *How Much is that Doggie in the Window* by Pattie Page; mine was *Why Don't You Do Right* by Peggy Lee. These were curious song choices for children stuck inside an oppressive religious family—we'd heard them on the car radio when dad & mom listened to sinful music outside the strict confines of Pentecostalism. They forgave themselves for this *tiny* sin, with the rationale that it was important research for creating their own catchy gospel music. It was typical Pentecostal behavior: I can sin—*you can't.*

Lard and Friends

Sharing an outhouse (and dirty bathwater) caused rashes to develop from time to time. Lard was known as the farmer's friend when it came to treating livestock skin disorders, and mom considered it good enough for us, too. Whenever crud showed up on our skin, mom slathered us in lard and said a prayer to Jesus. When the rash eventually disappeared, lard and prayer were both touted as cures.

The only upside to the farmhouse was when a stray dog befriended me there. She eventually had puppies, and even though she wasn't allowed in the house, I still considered her my friend. I was smart enough not to jinx her with a name though —I remembered what mom did to my pet chicken *Cock-a-Doodle-Doo.*

Country School

Once again I found myself in a new school: Country School, a single-building affair a half-mile down the road from the farmhouse. All of us attended: Lana (6th grade), me (3rd grade), and Gilbert (1st grade). Mark was still a toddler so he stayed home with mom.

One lesson in Country School discussed personal hygiene and the importance of keeping your teeth healthy, with our teacher demonstrating how to use a toothbrush. I'd never seen a toothbrush before, so upon returning home I asked mom why we didn't have one. Mom said they were only needed by adults. Being forever curious and assuming my parents had all the answers, I pressed mom for more information about why we didn't need a toothbrush. Mom eventually shut down my questioning, telling me that's just the way it was and stop asking questions.

Mom and dad never liked me asking questions because they knew I illuminated a harsh truth for them: They knew the real answers—they just didn't want to accept being wrong. I should have had a toothbrush.

Blizzards

With winter fast approaching, dad's religious fervor grew. I watched him transform every morning and night into the prayer position: crouched on his knees with eyes closed, head tilted to the heavens, hands clapping above his head. Dad would shake in the Spirit, tearfully begging Jesus to guide his life to its next destination. His prayers were always self-centered—he never asked Jesus to help his kids.

The blizzards that hit the farmhouse that winter in South Dakota were awful. The extreme cold made using the outhouse too dangerous, so we used a chamber pot instead. The chamber pot was white with a red-trimmed lid, and was located in the corner of an empty room that we used solely as a toilet. Mom instructed us to make sure we closed the lid real tight when we were done: In her words, "Like a jar of pickles."

I was old enough to know what was going on by now, and I wasn't happy with it. I held my nose every time I used the pot, and with six people in the house it was used a lot. Once the pot was full it had to be dumped outside, away from the house and our water well. This job fell to mom, who lugged the heavy pot outside and dumped our waste in a snowbank. At night, she'd do it in moonlight (since farms didn't have streetlights). I never saw exactly where it was dumped, so it was either shoveled over or covered by new snow. It was one question I knew not to ask—for fear of being assigned the *corrective* job of pot dumper.

Country School was mostly in-session during these blizzards, and mom insisted that we still had to *get up and get going.* While dad slept or prayed, mom packed lunches of hot creamed corn in a jar and sometimes a fried egg sandwich for us —a treat we truly loved. Happy daydreams of munching on fried-egg sandwiches quickly disappeared though, once we dressed for the dreadfully cold walk to school.

Three young lard-covered kids, faces covered with scarves to protect from frostbite, bent their bodies into the freezing wind and trudged towards the schoolhouse. The building wasn't even visible, we just moved down the road in the direction we knew it to be. Snow caked our eyelashes; Lips cracked and bled. By the time we covered the half-mile to school, our feet were frozen and our clothes soaked through. Inside the building, the first move was always to check for frostbite. I was royally pissed that my parents wouldn't just drop us off in the car and save us from this unnecessary pain.

Dad's Prayers Answered Again

After hundreds of prayers, and phone calls to Lyle & Albin, dad finally received word from *Jesus* that it was time to move. As it was, Country School only went to 6th grade and Lana was moving beyond that. Our destination—Brookings—was familiar to us. Only ten miles up the road, it's the same city where Lana and the first Janice Loy were born.

After our horrible life at the farmhouse, I was happy to finally leave it forever. That happiness was dashed when dad pulled out his rifle on our final day; Stray pets on a farm are *put down* when their humans abandon them, the rationale being that they'll suffer if people aren't around to feed them. Dad called my friend—the friendly stray dog—into the cornfield and shot her. He placed her puppies in a sack, tied it closed, and dunked them all in the river.

* * *

Our stay in Brookings was, like all of our previous moves, temporary. We didn't know that of course; Even though I'd figured out the gypsy routine by now, I still naively assumed that wherever we landed each time would be permanent. Regardless, I was thankful to be away from the cruel world of the Skovlund farm. Still top of mind was dad shooting my friend and drowning her puppies—together with mom murdering my pet chicken in Chisago City, these incidents made me a very pissed-off little girl.

Yet, I saw promise in my new home town. Brookings had sidewalks and paved roads, and a nice big school where I entered 4th grade and was introduced to the sinful art of *tap dancing*.

I knew dancing was a sin. Over and over through the years, my parents and everyone in their orbit explained how dancing led to sexual activity, but I was nine years old and sex was a foreign concept to me. Tap dancing wasn't foreign at all though, in fact it was immediately joyful. I loved clicking my little feet, and kept it very secret from my parents so they wouldn't put an end to the fun.

Chasing Sinners

While I secretly tapped away in class, dad was tearfully howling out to Jesus at home, pleading to the Lord for more guidance. Dad was obsessed with chasing down sinners all over South Dakota and was worried the Devil was winning the race for souls. It was really hard to endure his constant whining and praying, especially at night. I wondered why he couldn't just save the sinners in town? Our friendly neighbors in Chisago City, the ones who invited us over for *I Love Lucy*— why didn't he try to save them? Dad's all-consuming quest to save sinners always drove him *somewhere else*, making it impossible for our family to ever put down roots on a stable life.

Mom heard the same hysterical praying from dad, and after so many years with him, she knew what it meant: It was a signal—time to go. Once mom placed fresh paper bags in the house, we got the signal too. Within a week she'd write our names on the bags and pack them full. We'd form a line at the front door —bags in hand—awaiting dad's go-ahead to pile into the car and take our places for the drive. It was a well-practiced routine done many times before, and after only a few months in Brookings, it's just what we did. Our next stop was twenty miles down the road in Arlington, South Dakota, to hook up with Lyle who was starting a church. School for the kids—education—was unimportant. No more tap dancing for me.

* * *

Like dad, Lyle Lenning dragged his young family around the Midwest hunting sinners and, like dad, he was never successful at it. Lyle's latest effort in Arlington, South Dakota, was at the helm of a new Pentecostal church looking for a congregation. Since the Lennings & Rasmussens were always in contact over church business, Roy knew about Lyle's spiritual prospecting and offered to help get the church moving in the right direction.

Upon arrival, dad moved us into a small rental located behind a larger home, whose occupants we never saw. Our Arlington adventure was predictably short—about six months. We went to yet another school, attended yet another church (six days a week with Mondays off), made no friends of these strangers, and spun our wheels while dad spun his. However, two events from this time illustrate the hypocrisy of dad & mom's religious mania and how confusing it was to my curious mind.

Our family in South Dakota. We never stayed in one place too long.

Christian Cards

Ever since their days at North Central, Lyle & Roy (with Eunice & Elsie) enjoyed hanging out with each other, and while us kids weren't privy to their parties, we learned in Arlington that party time for them meant playing the card game *Rook*. Pentecostal rules strictly forbid card games, but somehow Rook became look-the-other-way acceptable—maybe because the cards replaced sinful Queens and Jokers with bland numbers and a bird. Now reunited in Arlington, the Lennings & Rasmussens resumed their card games at our small rental home. Dad even papered over the windows so church members couldn't peek in on Pastor Lyle—who preached that playing cards was a sin. It made no sense to me: If cards were forbidden, then why could dad & mom play with them, and if Rook was acceptable, then why did dad cover the windows? The whole thing was very confusing to me since it was so obviously *backwards*.

Far more troubling than Rook, however, was Lana's first date with dad's belt.

Lana Paints Her Lips

Along with a litany of other menial jobs, dad had long sold Fuller Brush kits door-to-door to generate income. And since we moved everywhere all the time, dad always had them in the trunk for quick sales. The kits contained a variety of personal hygiene and grooming tools—some even had makeup.

In the male-dominated world of 1950s Pentecostalism, using makeup was considered a very real sin. The men in these churches raged against dolled-up Hollywood stars, firmly believing that makeup alone would turn innocent young Christian girls into harlots working the streets of South Dakota.

Dad's Fuller Brush kits were full of lipsticks, rouges, and red nail polish—sinful temptations for young girls like me and Lana. One day we snuck a tube of red lipstick to try on. Lana went first, coating her lips red and enjoying the sinful pleasure of playing dress up. Suddenly, mom walked in the room and saw what we were up to. Horrified at the sight of her most obedient child's lips painted fire-engine red, mom angrily asked Lana why she'd broken the makeup rule. Lana's response was a firm denial: She hadn't broken the rule—*that was her natural lip color.*

Mom ran to inform dad as Lana chased behind, pleading that nothing was on her lips. Shocked by his daughter's blatant sinning, dad demanded that Lana tell the truth, but she continued lying about what was plain for all to see: Bright red lips burning with desire.

Dad's eyes lit up with rage at his sinful daughter. The belt we knew so well slid out from his pant loops and folded over for maximum control. I covered my ears while he hit her with it—I didn't want to hear Lana crying.

Even though I was young, I still knew my parents were holding us accountable to rules they ignored for themselves. If lipstick was sinful, why did we have it in the house? And why would dad *sell sin* to people he was trying to save?

Lana Never Caught a Break

Although Lana was always cold to us as adults (and secretive to a fault about our dad), she carried a heavy load in these earlier times. Whenever dad & mom went out with their goofball church friends (which was all the time), Lana was our babysitter. She was only a kid herself—thirteen years old in 1955—yet Gilbert, Mark, and me were dumped on her virtually every day. My parents were annoyingly selfish at Lana's expense; Life as the perfect child must have been miserable.

Wichita Calling

Just like Brookings, Arlington was over before it even began. Roy once again howled at the moon every night, and the moon delivered guidance in the form of brother Albin—the Human Onion. Albin was residing in Wichita and tipped Roy off that a *big-time church* in town needed a song leader; Albin had already lined the whole thing up, all Roy needed to do was show up for the formal interview.

For Roy, the only catch was that Wichita was further away from his parents than Brookings, or Arlington, or Minneapolis. Roy's four young children were growing, requiring more food to survive (and becoming more visible to the public if they were starving). Roy's financial lifeline wouldn't be so easy to grab from way down in Wichita, so before leaving he made a pit-stop at his parent's home in Bruce. After a few days of begging, baby Roy got what he wanted: cash from his parents and fresh wheels from brother Herman. Time to move.

* * *

Through the back window of our '54 Bel Air, I count stars in the night sky. One through one-hundred I count, keeping my math skills sharp for the day I get to attend school all the way through. One patch of sky finished, I focus on a new one—the stars high above rural roads are as endless as the drive.

My bed atop the car's rear deck is my comfort zone, the stars my stability—they never moved, perfectly happy to remain where they were forever. Not like my dad, who couldn't stay in one place for more than a year before throwing our lives into chaos again.

From the very beginning, mom told me I could have the back window because I was special. I was surprised she felt that way about me—and I loved my bed there —but I knew she only wanted my questioning mouth away from her and dad's religious ears. Perched on the Bel Air's rear deck, I couldn't be any further from them unless they placed me in the trunk.

Even though I looked like a hungry orphan pulled from *The Boxcar Children,* I still had a lot of pride in myself. We traveled so often that the car was our home for days at a time; Lana and I knew the pee protocol from our Central Valley days and taught it to the boys: Go behind the right-rear tire and watch your shoes so they don't get wet. We knew our seat positions: Lana had the backseat left side, Gilbert had the right, I had the rear-window perch, and little Mark sat up front with mom. Dad was friendly with Mark, sometimes allowing him to play drive.

The long drives were relentlessly boring. Farmland, barns, big trees and the occasional deserted building that slowly approached before receding behind us. After a couple hours driving down Midwestern highways, everything blends into a dull beige blur. Dad cut the boredom by practicing scales, but the novelty of that had long worn off for me. The best we'd get was scratchy music on the radio, but that was just another confusing hypocrisy since Pentecostals weren't allowed to listen to music. I presume dad's excuse was that he needed melodies to use in church.

The highway sign declaring Wichita's boundaries finally arrived and dad pulled out a map to search for Albin & Evelyn's house. They'd recently relocated, having previously lived in a trailer Albin owned in nearby Haysville. Dad planned to park us at Albin's house until he secured the song leader job, then move us into Albin's trailer for more rent-free living. In the best of times it was a shortsighted plan, but our times were always bad—dad's plan would soon make life worse.

WICHITA NIGHTMARE

Pastor Wallace—first name unknown—stood at the helm of Wichita's biggest Pentecostal church. Short and fat, he was also missing his right thumb. The official explanation was that it was shot off in the war, but considering Pentecostalism's shady cast of characters in the 40s and 50s, perhaps he got caught cheating at poker and had to pay his debt. After all, honest men never make good preachers.

Pastor Wallace's church was in desperate need of a song leader: The guy who sparks up the congregation for a half-hour until people are good and ready to give to the Lord—at which time the Pastor arrives to facilitate the giving. If the Pastor has a guest or wants to go long, the song leader steps in again to keep the mood elevated and passions high. Tongues were inevitable in Pentecostal services, but they couldn't come out without being warmed up first. Pentecostal tongue-madness looks spontaneous on the surface, but getting there is a well-controlled process akin to a pre-game warmup in athletics—go in with tongues cold and you risk injury.

Roy's guitar skill, exotic outsider status, and the general lack of participation among Wichita's *actual musicians* all placed him in the winner's circle for Pastor Wallace. Roy's high nasal voice, the steady-worsening eye blink, even his rubber-banded shirt sleeves didn't matter to Wallace. Roy applied, he was competent, and there were no other candidates for the position. The job was his for the taking.

Though the song leader role diverged from Roy's save-every-soul-in-America mission, it still granted him a respected seat on stage—one without any of the dreaded Pastoral responsibilities. The position had no growth potential since song leaders will never inherit the throne, but it offered pride and a tiny stipend. And maybe it would lead to other opportunities down the road.

Both men satisfied with the other, Roy and Wallace sealed the deal with what must have been a very awkward handshake.

Song Leader Roy (pictured at Albin's house)

Bizarre Trailer Park

Church job secured, dad proceeded to the final step of his grand Wichita plan: moving us into Albin's Haysville trailer, ten miles outside of town.

Incorporated in 1951, Haysville—emphasis on *hay*—was a town of five-thousand humans who'd only recently learned how to govern themselves when we arrived in 1955. Albin's trailer was nowhere near those humans though, instead it was parked in the strangest location I've ever seen—a tiny community of trailers living at the bottom of a highway turnoff where the *we're a city now* message was yet to be received.

Part bomb-crater and part UFO-landing-pad, the trailer park was formed in a literal dustbowl set steeply down from the highway. The manager's house sat at the bottom of the entrance road, though there wasn't much to manage—the only amenities were tall tower lights (like a sports field) and a concrete bunker containing the community bathroom.

This place had no reason to exist. The severe slope off the highway caused runoff that turned it muddy in the rain. Nights were pitch black once the tower lights turned off. The location was completely uninhabitable—except for the fact that people actually lived here.

The idea that someone would carve a giant crater out of the ground for folks to live in trailers made no sense whatsoever. What made far more sense—especially considering the bizarre concrete bunker—was that this place was used as target practice for nearby US pilots during World War Two. As a result, the crater already existed, as did the concrete bunker. A decade later, an enterprising Haysville local decided to repurpose the crater and it's bunker. Most bizarre of all was that it worked—people arrived with their trailers. People like Albin, and now people like us.

Once we set eyes on Albin's trailer, we immediately understood why he moved to a house. It was a small aluminum travel trailer on wheels—27 feet long, 10 feet wide—something that modern people would tow on a camping weekend. In 1955, we made it a home for six people.

A cinder block at the side-entry door served as a step into our tiny new world. Inside was a single open area with adult sleeping-quarters hidden behind a pocket door. Albin cleaned nothing before leaving: Discards littered the floor and the walls were stained with grease, perhaps by Evelyn who, at over 300 pounds, must have constantly scraped against them. The kitchenette had a small sink, stove, and fridge. Water was provided by an external tank attached to the trailer's body; Electricity magically came from *somewhere,* as it always does.

There was no bathroom in the trailer. Day or night, rain or snow, we walked to the bunker and used a stall every time nature called. The bunker had showers too, but we never used them since dad & mom quickly figured out how to bathe in the kitchen sink: A privacy curtain was nailed to the ceiling, and on Sunday mornings we lined up to take turns sponging ourselves clean. Dad always went first.

The open living area had no drawers or closets for storage, so clothing was kept in our trusty paper bags sat neatly by the door: *Lana–Janice–Gilbert–Mark.* A table pulled down from the wall and mated with a fixed wood bench during daylight hours; At night, the table went up and the hard wood bench became a bed for me and Lana, who slept feet-to-feet. Gilbert and Mark slept feet-to-feet too—on an army cot that mom kept in the car trunk for situations like this.

Mom provided blankets to keep us warm, she even fluffed our pillows every night —a loving gesture to make us more comfortable. She knew things weren't going well.

Nutrition was spotty and alternated between egg sandwiches, bread with ketchup, or toast with hot milk & sugar. Tornados were very scary—when they came through, we fled to Albin's house to take shelter in his storm cellar.

Since the crater lights went off at 9pm, illumination inside the trailer was by candle light. It was then—while we lay on our benches and cots—that mom whispered a reminder to say our prayers. "You're lucky little tykes," she reassured us. "Poor families have it much worse than this. Some have no place at all."

Settling In

I was constantly embarrassed for my parents and our living arrangements, and of all the horrible places we'd lived up to that point, Albin's trailer was the worst. The Skovlund's farmhouse was awful, but it had the charm of independence. Albin's dirty trailer, on the other hand, always carried his stench—you couldn't breathe without being reminded that Albin owned our air. Nevertheless, it was still better than living in the car.

After a few weeks, dad settled in to the song leader job. Since the position was virtually unpaid (a small stipend plus a tiny share of offerings), he sold vacuums for Sears again, in addition to his dependable door-to-door sales of religious paraphernalia.

Out of the blue, mom suddenly took an interest in our education. Maybe she finally realized how many times we'd moved in the last five years; Maybe she thought getting us in school would finally anchor Roy to a location for good. Her official reason was that she *didn't want to see our education suffer*—implying that she knew it was suffering. The result of her epiphany was that all of us were quickly enrolled in the Haysville school system. That's where I met Mr Guthrie—a pervert teacher who liked to swat bottoms.

Mr Guthrie's Special Birthday Gift

Fifth-grade teacher Mr. Guthrie—dark hair, large Adam's Apple, booming voice— had a long leather sleeve hanging on the wall behind his desk. I knew what was in that sleeve: A paddle, used to discipline kids who misbehaved on the playground. What I didn't know was that Mr Guthrie also used the paddle for pleasure—his own. Children in Mr Guthrie's class got swatted on their birthdays—they looked forward to it—but since I was new to his class (and the school), I was unaware of Mr Guthrie's special birthday gift.

My birthday came around and Mr Guthrie called me to the front of class. Mr Guthrie's shadowy features and deep voice always frightened me, but since I was his student and he was my teacher, I complied. My classmates giggled in anticipation: They'd already endured the paddle, now it was my turn.

Mr Guthrie instructed me to bend over his desk. I nervously assumed the position and watched Mr Guthrie move to the wall and remove the paddle from its sleeve. Mr Guthrie casually walked behind me and out of view—the last thing I saw was Adam's Apple.

"How old are you today, Janice?" Mr Guthrie's voice boomed.

"Eleven," I answered.

Suddenly, the paddle hit my backside. I stared at the chalkboard, confused as to why I was being punished. Mr Guthrie hit me again—this time harder. The mixed laughter of children and Guthrie reached my ears as I wondered what the hell was going on.

"Three!" cheered the class as Mr Guthrie smacked me again. "Four!" The painful swats continued as my eyes filled up. "Five, six, seven," the kids laughed, all the way to eleven.

"And one more for good luck!" announced a now-breathless Guthrie while delivering the hardest swat. "Alright Janice, *you're all done.*"

I turned around and saw the entire class in hysterics. Mr Guthrie—Adam's Apple bobbing inside his neck—boomed his congratulations, "Happy Birthday!"

During recess, I went in the bathroom and cried. The shock of bending over Mr Guthrie's desk while he paddled me to the laughter of classmates was humiliating. When I got home, I told mom what happened and showed her my bruises. In a surprising gesture of concern, dad & mom met with the Principal to complain about Mr Guthrie. Nothing happened of course—the paddle was completely normal in 1950s Wichita. Even for perverts.

The Bus Room

School in Haysville offered much better moments than Mr Guthrie. Those moments happened in the bus room.

The bus room was where students waited after school for their bus route to be called over the intercom. The long spans of time spent waiting between callouts was magical, since that's when the normal person manning the intercom played radio hits. *Rock Around the Clock, Earth Angel, Mr Sandman,* and more were played— thrilling songs with toe-tapping beats that tickled my ears. It was fun and exciting, sweeping me away to a much nicer world than the one I was forced to live in. None of the songs mentioned Jesus or the Bible, and the characters weren't poor, hungry people living in a trailer without a toilet. Those beautiful songs were the only thing that ever gave me hope—I'd spend my whole life in that bus room if I could.

* * *

After a few months spent easing into Haysville life, Albin informed dad that he needed the trailer back. Fred Lenning—wife-spanking ringleader of the Lenning-Rasmussen circus—played up California's church prospects to Albin, specifically those in Long Beach, so Albin decided to move there. That meant towing away the trailer *without us in it.* I didn't like the trailer—nobody liked it except dad since it was free—but uprooting ourselves again, including going to yet another new school, never felt good.

As a child, it seemed to me that the sky could fall at any time, because it did—over and over the stable world consistently crashed in on us. Albin kicking us out was further evidence that it was only a matter of time before the world would turn upside-down again. It always did.

Little Princess

Evicted from Albin's Haysville trailer, dad secured new lodging for us at a Wichita residential motel with weekly rates. Even though it was the smallest of the motel's apartments, the room was a huge improvement over the trailer since it had a working toilet and semblance of normalcy.

My new school was also a step up from Haysville because it offered children the chance to work for food: Child labor was used to wash the lunch trays, and in return the laborers were given free lunch to close the loop on this curiously efficient operation. I was accepted into the program and felt very proud to contribute to our family by saving us money. The cherry on top was the hairnet I got to wear—I felt like a little princess.

Lana Branches Out

Our Wichita school was close to the motel, so I could walk home each day with Gilbert instead of waiting for the school bus. Mom and dad weren't home after school—they roamed the city with Mark all day, selling bibles and Jesus pictures. Without parents around in the afternoon, Gilbert and I could sit on the floor in peace, playing *Jax* and listening to the radio.

Lana, on the other hand, was playing something far worse than *Jax*. She'd taken up a secret life with Danny Wallace—the twenty-year-old son of dad's boss, Pastor Wallace. Their pimply relationship would soon come to a head, but while it secretly grew below the surface, our family tended to the most pressing issue of the day: church attendance.

Standing in front of Albin's house, ready for church.

Church Life

Church was (and had always been) six days a week with Mondays off. On the free night, dad attended local camp meetings—sometimes with Gilbert—to watch Oral Roberts and other high-profile preachers put on a show. He was forever on the run for Jesus—everyone else be damned. You'd never find dad sat at a dinner table asking us about school because dad's only interests were Jesus and himself— sometimes I wondered if he even knew my name.

Weekday church services by junior preachers were an extremely boring time since they required sitting down and listening to uninteresting topics. Even mom got bored and took to inspecting our ears for dirt: If any was found, she'd spit on a tissue and clean it out. Dad's praise songs—simple sing-along hymns for a simple congregation—gave us a chance to use our voices and stretch, but the sermon parts of the services were agonizingly dull. By night's end I'd find myself laying at mom's feet, spying under the pews to see which church member had littered.

Pastor Wallace's sermons were different though; On Sundays and other days when Wallace took the pulpit, he preached a sci-fi sermon filled with communists and nuclear war and taking shelter in the mountains for the End Times—basically a Christian reworking of 1950s government propaganda.

UFOs were a big deal in the United States in 1956, especially the Midwest. The disturbing sightings of mysterious flying ships—the threat of foreign invaders—was perfect for ratcheting up the national mood. Pastor Wallace dutifully equated UFOs with Russians in his sermons, warning that they'd soon drop a bomb on downtown Wichita. Some might argue that Wichita wouldn't be missed, but for those of us living there it was a terrifying prospect. Pastor Wallace preached that the bombs would rain terror down on all of us, so we must stock our cars with food and water in preparation for survival. When—not if—the day came, our orders were to head for the hills. From God's mouth to our American ears.

The Destruction of Wichita

Forced to hear these doom-filled sermons time and again for weeks, I eventually cracked—a crying spell hit me during dad's song service. Mom shushed me but I wouldn't stop crying, explaining to mom that I saw something scary projected on the church's rear wall: I saw the destruction of Wichita.

> Excited that her young daughter's finally embracing Pentecost, Elsie signals to Roy that something groundbreaking is happening with Janice. Roy halts the song service with an announcement: His daughter's just received a vision.
>
> Mom escorts me to the foot of the stage. From there, father leads me by the hand.
>
> "Come right up here, Janice. Stand on this stool and tell everyone what you saw."
>
> *He knows my name.*
>
> I mount the stool and lean in to the microphone. It's at this moment —right before speaking—that I realize the entire church's attention

is on me. I look over at dad and see him looking back—I have his attention, too.

"Don't be scared Janice. Tell everyone your vision."

My lips quiver as tears roll down my cheeks. "I'm scared that the UFOs and bombs are going to destroy Wichita and we're all gonna die. I watched it happen on that wall back there."

I point to the rear of the church; Fat-bodied simpletons track my finger, twisting and craning their necks to view the church's phlegm-colored rear wall. A few linger on the wall, hoping to receive their own vision.

I add an extra detail to my prophecy: "Jesus said if we find a thousand Christians in Wichita, the city will be spared."

The congregation rise to their feet to celebrate my message of mercy. Flabby arms reach for the heavens as tongues fly free. I cease crying; That was only for attention and now I'm getting more than I've ever had, including from the person I wanted it from most—dad's eyes meet mine with a smile.

At eleven years old, I didn't know that the cause of my spooky daydream was Pastor Wallace's unrelenting Apocalypse sermons—that I was simply regurgitating what I'd heard for weeks on end, and filling in the blanks with Jesus. Had I known, I wouldn't have cared anyways. My dad was proud of me and the church gave me a standing ovation. I felt like a superstar: Shirley Temple without the curls.

* * *

With dad's star rising, he moved us to better digs—the motel's end-unit apartment. This larger apartment had a bedroom and kitchen, plus a perfect view down the street of the local drive-in's huge screen that showed nightly movies featuring beautiful actresses like Kim Novak and Gina Lollobrigida. We often played on the apartment's front steps, and although mom sternly instructed us to keep our eyes closed to the sinful movies that played, it was impossible not to peek.

The escape of the movie screen provided us with some joyful moments, but that pleasure was soon balanced out by the pain of Lana's arguments with dad & mom. Completely out-of-character, quiet Lana was now loudly asserting herself and attempting to flee her torturous life by running off with Danny Wallace. Being the son of Pastor Wallace, Danny had a solid family pedigree, but he was twenty years old and Lana was fourteen, so they needed a signed court petition to get married. Dad and mom refused to sign.

Their arguments carried on for days. Lana—the perfect child who never questioned her parents—was now yelling at them and causing a major scene. I'd sit on the front step covering my ears to escape the disturbing screams, but it never worked. After it was finally over—left unresolved—I knew a line had been crossed and we'd all pay the price for it.

After those arguments, tensions rose in our family. One Sunday morning while loading in the car for church, three-year-old Mark had to pee and chose to use a bush outside our motel room. Dad angrily exited the car, pulled Mark into the apartment, and belted him. Again I heard screaming; again I covered my ears.

Blinking Intensifies

Dad's eyes always had an odd blink, but now the blink was worsening. He began having terrible headaches accompanied with blindness, and sometimes the headaches caused him to vomit. I was very concerned when these spells hit him, but when I asked mom if he was okay she'd tell me to quit talking because it hurt his head to hear me. I learned to just go outside and zip my lip—my questions were too much for them.

Dad even sought a doctor about his head—a first for him. The doctor identified food allergies as the cause of his headaches, advising dad to improve his diet and avoid consuming caffeine, wheat bread, and nuts. A *more-balanced diet* was impossible for dad on his tiny income, but it wouldn't have mattered anyways—Jesus planted an aneurysm in his head and would soon call him home. Nuts or no nuts.

Food Showers

With screaming headaches and a screaming teenage daughter, the pressure on dad was enormous. The final straw was when the good people of Wichita threw food showers for their beloved song leader Roy. They noticed the tattered clothes and tight bellies of his pale children. They knew the six of us all lived in a motel down the street. They wanted to help us—wanted us to get better. They wanted us to stay. *Jesus extended His hand.*

Dad was having none of it. He was extremely upset that these people—kind people —had the nerve to put grocery bags filled with food in his car. According to mom, the first time it happened he laid across the bed sobbing while she patted his head. "Who do these people think they are?" he cried. Matilda's little boy was embarrassed.

The weekly food showers continued, and each time dad angrily ranted that we didn't need food or charity. He couldn't see the poor condition his kids were in —all he saw was himself. We were hungry—always hungry—yet his unwavering mission was to save everyone *but us*. If other people tried to save us, to hell with them—he'd sooner quit then be humiliated.

On the Road Again

Roy spoke to Fred & Albin and all agreed that Long Beach was the promised land. Maybe Roy factored his health into the equation, wanting to park his family in a safer town in case something happened to him. Or maybe he just thought Wichita had become another dead end for him—he'd saved all the sinners and now they turned around and tried to save him. How dare they: *Roy Rasmussen didn't need saving.*

Lana going off-the-rails was also a major issue. She turned face so swiftly on her parents that they knew she could no longer be trusted. Danny Wallace had a car, and every new day they spent in Wichita was a day she might not come home.

Four fresh paper bags were packed and labeled: *Lana–Janice–Gilbert–Mark.* We grabbed our assignments and loaded up in the Bel Air. In dad's rush to leave, he left his guitar case on the ground behind the car. Backing out of the driveway, he ran over it—destroying the guitar inside.

On our long drive out to Long Beach, Lana asked if we could stop and see the Grand Canyon. Dad declined, saying it would take too long. He wanted to reach Long Beach as fast as possible. Maybe it was his health after all.

JUNE 1957: OFF THE RAILS

I sat quietly with Lana as the train rumbled along on its journey from Los Angeles to Sioux Falls. Traveling alone with Lana was intimidating enough—if she didn't bite us with teeth, she bit us with words—but now I had adult passengers to watch out for. Tall men, short men, hairy men, fat men—all wore suits and all reeked of alcohol. However bad my dad may have smelled, he never smelled like them— Pentecostals were proudly teetotal, to the extent that mom's lifelong claim-to-fame was that liquor never touched her tongue. That was the victory she celebrated.

Dad was gone now, and mom was nowhere to be found. For the next few days it was just me and Lana—together alone—on a train to Sioux Falls. On arrival, we'd be met by dad's brother Herman and Aunt Lorraine. Or so we hoped.

Friendly Faces

Tired and hungry, our train arrived after dark in Sioux Falls, where Uncle Herman & Aunt Lorraine waited with warm smiles and open arms. They were unobtrusive Lutherans—much nicer people than obnoxious Pentecostals like dad and Albin, who were constantly in your face with Jesus. Uncle Herman, friendly and strong, loaded us into his dealership car and off we went to Bruce—together as family.

Between Albin & Evelyn's custody and the train ride with Lana, I'd felt very alone for the last few months, but cousins Karen & Lois gave me acceptance. In my tattered clothes, I must have looked like a pitiful orphan—and without parents, I was—but to them I was just cousin Janice. With Aunt Lorraine's urging, they gave Lana and me lots of nice hand-me-downs to wear.

Over the next few days, Aunt Lorraine fed us and ran hot water for our baths, doing everything she could to allow peaceful recuperation. We even went on a picnic together—a nice carefree adventure to help heal our sad hearts. The whole family was compassionate and didn't want us suffering any more than we already had. Decades later, Aunt Lorraine visited me in Long Beach, where I told her how grateful I was for her love and kindness. She sat in front of me and cried.

Uncle Herman & Aunt Lorraine, who cried in front of me years later.

* * *

Dad's death fragmented our tight family unit, and that fragmentation continued after arriving back in the Midwest. Lana was sent to Uncle Haaken & Aunt Esther's house in Bruce, and I was headed down the road to Estelline, South Dakota, with Uncle Philip & Aunt Phyllis. Where mom and my brothers were, I had no clue.

Mom's breakdown after dad's death was treated with heavy doses of *Librium*. Unable to compose herself, she was sent to Detroit (along with young Mark and Gilbert) to recuperate over the summer with Bill & Joyce Leigh—close friends from North Central. Mark remained with mom but Gilbert was immediately sent to Holt, Michigan, to finish out the school year with Aunt Evelyn & Don Smith.

This fragmentation was head-spinning, most of all for us inside it. The Rasmussen clan sprang to action after their baby brother's death, but discussions between them are lost to time. Ideally we'd be kept together rather than split apart, but who'd have room for five more people? We did it once before at Grandpa & Grandma Rasmussen's farm, but Grandma Matilda died two months before Roy—even for an indomitable man like Grandpa Gilbert, taking on his dead son's family was too much. The idea of adopting us may have been floated, with each of us going to an aunt or uncle to see if we fit. It was, after all, where we found ourselves now. Or perhaps the fragmentation was simply to give Elsie respite: Time without responsibility, time among friends to strengthen her mind for whatever came next.

Those thoughts were impossible for me then, and that was good. At present, I had Aunt Lorraine's warmth and Uncle Herman's safety, and they reassured me that I'd love staying in Estelline with Philip & Phyllis, and my older cousin Sharon. I felt good about it. *I was ready.*

Estelline

It was in Estelline where I met the sweetest lamb in all of South Dakota. Uncle Philip & Aunt Phyllis sensed how much I needed something to care for, so they gave me one in Lami—a baby lamb who occupied their front yard. They handed me a bottle and asked me to feed her, a task I loved from the very first second. When Lami saw me coming with the bottle she made squeaking sounds—I patted her little head while she drank from my hand. Lami was sweet sugar for my lonely heart, and Philip & Phyllis were so kind to give me those eternally happy moments with her.

Uncle Philip & Aunt Phyllis gave me the sweetest lamb in all of South Dakota.

The Lord giveth and the Lord taketh away—the utter joy I experienced with Lami was balanced out by the horror of my first period. I'd never been taught about menstruation, so seeing my own blood frightened me—I thought I would die like dad. Cousin Sharon reassured me that I wasn't dying, but it was an unfortunately timed event that brought dad's death back to mind when I was still very fragile.

With June becoming July, our family's reunification began—mom and my brothers would soon arrive in Bruce to stay at Grandpa Rasmussen's farm. Lana and I would stay put for the time being, but since the distance between Estelline and Bruce was close, spending time together would be easy.

I had mixed feelings about seeing mom again. The last time I'd seen her she was a complete wreck of tears and sadness, and my gut told me she hadn't changed. I wasn't sure if I could endure her depression and constant crying; I wasn't even sure if she'd recognize me.

My brothers were a different story—I looked forward to being back with them. I wanted to see how much Mark had grown, and have fun conversations with Gilbert; I wanted the three of us to play together again. Lana didn't factor into our mix since she was off doing her own thing with Uncle Haaken's married daughter, cousin Darlene.

The first big event after reuniting was on the Fourth of July when we celebrated Mark's 5th birthday with Phillip & Phyllis, who moved the celebration up a few days to coincide with the town's fireworks display. They prepared a picnic for us, baked a cake with candles—they even had birthday presents. Mark's huge smile said it all, yet one person was still unable to celebrate: Mom, who remained emotionally vacant and distant. She smiled reflexively for cameras, but mom's *Librium*-treated grief turned her into a sad zombie that nobody wanted to be around.

* * *

During a family hangout at Grandpa's farm, we got together with our cousins to play outside as the gloomy adults visited indoors. We overheard serious conversations and lots of crying coming from the house, so we escaped the noise by racing over to Grandpa's barn—the place where fun always happened.

We decided to play hide-and-seek way up in the hayloft—15-feet off the ground—something we'd done many times before. The loft had two ways to enter: A ladder inside the barn, and an outside rope affixed to the top of the barn that hung all the way to the ground. Those who used the rope didn't climb it, instead they held on tight while someone in the loft pulled them up.

Being hauled up on the rope wasn't hard for lightweight little kids: Grab the rope, hold on tight, then ten seconds later you're in the loft. Mark, brimming with the naive confidence of a newly crowned five year old, saw the fun we had on the rope and decided he wanted to do it too. He grabbed the rope, and in a tiny voice yelled to the hayloft, "Pull me up!"

Mark's feet left the ground and he giggled at the feeling of being hauled into the air. Higher and higher he went, experiencing a view of the world he'd never had before. "This five-year-old stuff is pretty cool," Mark thought. He looked up to the loft and saw us looking down, only a few feet away from him. "I'm going again after this one," he thought. Then he lost his grip.

Mark hit the ground with a thud. We looked down at his motionless little body—we thought we'd lost another Rasmussen. Nobody dared breathe as we watched for movement. After a few seconds, he finally sat up. The fall knocked the wind out of him—it knocked the wind out of us too—but otherwise he was fine. Mark brushed himself off and took the ladder up to the loft, where we finally started our game of hide-and-seek among the hay bales.

We chased each other for hours in that big red barn—innocent giggles and screams rising to the heavens—until the sun set on our fun and it was time to go. We were leaving for good this time: Mom was taking us to Lansing, Michigan, to stay with Aunt Evelyn & Don Smith. Tears fell as we said goodbye to our cousins, our aunts & uncles, and our dear Grandpa Gilbert—the man who gave so much and took so little. Grandpa and his farm would exist only in memories from that point on. They were good ones.

MICHIGAN SUMMER

Evelyn Smith—dad's sister—was my favorite aunt. Too glamorous and fun for Lansing, she wore makeup and earrings, fashionable clothes, and didn't take no for an answer. She was Lutheran like all the Rasmussens (except Albin and Roy), which meant she had no weird hangups. Aunt Evelyn once surprised me with a gift from her department store job: A perfect blue dress that highlighted my blonde Norwegian hair. I felt like a princess in that dress one who could conquer the world. Evelyn's kindness and savvy gave me confidence at a time when I needed it most. She knew *exactly* what she was doing.

Evelyn's husband Don was a nice, quiet man, the perfect counterpoint to Evelyn. Unfortunately, I cried when I was around him too much—his presence made me realize I didn't have a dad anymore. That wasn't Don's fault.

Crying fits aside, Don & Evelyn were great fun. They took us to a lake with a dock at its center; We'd swim out to the dock and practice diving from it. When the sun went down, we roasted hot dogs and loaded them with mustard and ketchup. We did all the things we never experienced with our own parents, who locked us away in a Pentecostal prison where worldly fun was prohibited at all times.

Lana was in the car with us to Lansing, but once we arrived I never saw her again. It seemed that nobody ever worried about Lana but me—perhaps I fixated on everyone's location for fear of losing them.

Don & Evelyn frequently took their four children to the movies. They also drank alcohol. These were major sins in Pentecostalism, and mom was very unhappy knowing how close sin was to her children. The Smiths, to their credit, didn't advertise these sins to us; They never invited us to the movies, not that we would have gone anyways—the Wichita drive-in experience had already trained us to close our eyes to movie sin.

The tension among adults in the house was thick. We were guests—refugees—in their home, but mom disapproved of their behavior and hid from it by isolating herself in a bedroom. The Smiths, in turn, saw a broken woman and her broken children being *further broken* by the religion she clinged to. Mom prayed for our souls every night—including those of the sinful Smith family. The Smiths reciprocated by feeding and bathing us. Who was the sinner and who was the saint?

The Smith's had a son named Roger who was the same age as Gilbert, and the same height—short. Since Gilbert previously lived with the Smith family for a few weeks after leaving Long Beach, the boys already had a history with each other. Whatever that history was, their present relationship consisted of fist fights. Nobody wants fighting in their home—much less fighting from a guest—and the boys' constant bickering set a clock ticking in the mind of Don Smith. Elsie and her fatherless children were never meant to stay forever, but increasing tensions ensured that the stay would be brief.

* * *

Five-year-old Mark Rasmussen suddenly realizes he's naked in front of the Lord. He hadn't eaten any forbidden apples—though he did have applesauce for lunch. He now sits bare-bottomed in the Smith's kitchen sink as relatives wander about. Warm water pours over his head; through bubbles, he makes out mom's face. She scrubs his ears.

"This is really weird," Mark vocalizes in his head.

Aunt Evelyn reaches above his head to open a cupboard. He quickly covers up as she removes a plate.

Mom readies another cup of water. "Close your eyes," she instructs Mark.

"You close yours!" his internal voice replies.

Warm water washes more soapy residue down his face; Mark sees mom more clearly now. An eerie, frozen smile paints her face—is she pretending to wash me? He's never, ever sat naked in someone else's sink, certainly not at mid-day with people around. And they're eating.

In the front yard, Gilbert and Roger stand face-to-face, measuring the tops of each others' heads.

"I'm taller!" yells Gilbert.

"No I'm taller!" Roger yells back.

"Wanna bet!?"

Don Smith hastily leaves the dining room to intervene. The boys grunt and wrestle each other as Mark watches through the kitchen window. More warm water washes over his head. His eyes sting.

"Boys, come inside and have some pie!" Aunt Evelyn hollers.

Cousin Susan, eleven years old, approaches the sink. Embarrassed to be seen flesh whole, Mark covers up again.

"Cute boy, Mark!" she smiles, placing her drinking glass under the faucet for a fill up. Mark leans forward to give her room. He glances at mom—her face is still frozen in that weird grin.

"I wish mom would stop smiling like that!" he pleads internally. "And why am I sitting naked in this sink!?"

As the relatives laugh and eat, Elsie continues washing her son for all the world to see.

Mom never showed an interest in our hygiene, so maybe the bizarre Mark-washing episode was an awkward attempt to show others that she was capable of parenting again. That didn't make Mark feel any better; the vivid memory of being naked for everyone to see was imprinted on his mind forever. But this weird event coupled with our fist-fighting brother tested poor Don & Evelyn's patience, and though we weren't asked to leave, we knew it was time to go. They were very nice to us —everyone was—but Pentecostals only fit with their own kind, and mom had her eyes set on Detroit. She'd already tested the waters there with North Central friends Bill & Joyce Leigh—now she was diving in.

* * *

I was glad to finally leave the tension of Don & Evelyn's home and board a train to Detroit. The ride wasn't long and our whole family was together for it. We arrived to the home of Bill & Joyce Leigh, Pentecostals who knew how to have live life without too much prohibition. They weren't relatives, but that sort of thing never mattered to me—nice people are nice people.

Being August in Detroit, my brothers and I played outside most of the time. I'd pretend to be a queen and make them bow to me as servants, or direct their moves

Bill & Joyce Leigh, friends from the Bible Institute and good people.

in a laughter-filled game of hide-and-seek. Over the last few years I'd unwittingly inherited authority over them—a surrogate mother role—and though we all laughed now, the fun would end in the not-too-distant future when my mother role went from voluntary to mandated.

The three of us—Gilbert, Mark, and me—began feeling good about Detroit. We had food on a regular basis courtesy of Bill & Joyce, who also took us around to parks and lakes for recreation. We went to their downtown church, where I made friends with two sisters who were my age. The sisters even invited me to lunch in their home, where I tasted rice & beans for the first time.

Lana, however, didn't like Detroit at all. We never saw her until we did, and those times weren't pleasant. She was now a crabby fifteen year old who insisted to mom that she was heading to Fort Wayne, Indiana, to visit her married cousin Darlene —no matter what. Mom argued with her over it, but I could see that mom was weak and Lana was rising. Lana eventually got her way and boarded a bus to Indiana. I was glad she left and hoped she wouldn't return.

By the middle of August—with the school year fast approaching—mom needed to choose where our final home would be: Would we return to Long Beach, or would we stay in Detroit?

Long Beach offered Albin & Big Evelyn, Lyle & Eunice, great weather, and one enormously bad memory. Detroit's winter weather was terribly familiar to us, but mom had true friends in Joyce & Bill, plus a strong new acquaintance in Sister Beale—the fat-on-fried-food leader of Detroit's Latter Rain Pentecostal church.

Without employment or money, and with no family relations of her own, living in a town with trusted friends nearby was of utmost importance to mom. Albin Rasmussen wasn't blood, and he was disagreeable as a person. Lyle Lenning was a good man, but also not a blood relation. How far would they really go to help a broken widow?

Mom's choice was made. We'd stay in Detroit.

* * *

We weren't happy when Lana returned from Indiana. She was quiet—brooding —and when she lashed out, any one of us could get bit. Lana was very much a reflection of Alfred Thompson—the grandfather who crossed the street to avoid his own grandchildren. When Lana learned we were staying in Detroit, she exploded.

Lana was determined to get back to Long Beach and be with her cousins (and teenage boys) at Bethany Chapel. Detroit offered her nothing but freezing weather and long bus rides to Indiana. Mom stood up to her—the choice was made—but Lana was a Viking. None of us would dare challenge mom's rule like Lana did, nor would we dare challenge Lana. We steered far clear of their arguments—we only wanted the fighting to stop.

In Wichita, Lana fought both mom *and* dad over Danny Wallace, and she didn't lose—dad just moved our family away from the problem. Now Lana had one less person to battle against. Throughout our lives, mom's will was iron. Unbending. *Lana bent it.* We were headed back to Long Beach.

Part II

Andy

LONG BEACH: NEW BEGINNINGS

The best thing Lana ever did for our family was get us the hell out of Detroit and the Midwest. Whatever our future would have been there, it's undoubtedly worse than the future Long Beach had in store for us—even in light of the turmoil to come. Lana's choice wasn't made for family though—it was made for herself. We were a losing proposition, and Lana knew if she remained with the sheep, she'd get the slaughter.

While dad was alive, Lana previewed the endless opportunities offered by Long Beach—especially the boys. The Midwest, by comparison, held only a lifetime of dead ends. Lana recognized the endless cycle of rebirth that kept turning us into the same poor people living in a new poor town, and she figured out how to escape it: *Marriage*. Long Beach was the end of the line for Lana. No more train rides.

Two Left Feet

When we first landed back in Long Beach, the local network of Rasmussens and Lennings were very kind to us. They got us moved into an upstairs apartment on Hellman Street, where we were neighbors once again with the Huskas (as well as Uncle Lorelle's family). Family helped mom apply for social security benefits, and many boxes of clothing were donated to us. One of those boxes contained tennis shoes around my size—just what I needed for junior high.

Starting junior high was a big deal for me. Gym class was a new experience and I was super excited when the teacher told us we needed tennis shoes for class. I'd never owned a pair—all my previous shoes were dressy hand-me-downs that never quite fit right—so I was jazzed to try on the cool tennis shoes donated to me by family.

If it wasn't fate's cruel joke, then it was a relative who decided that two left shoes were better than none. The left one fit fine—obviously—but my right foot was crammed inside and straining in vain against everything the shoe was made to do. Human feet are not table legs; They have arches and curves and five different toes. Millions of years of evolution—*or six days of divine work*—fought against that shoe, but the damn thing wouldn't budge.

The shoe was the shoe, and at this point there was no going back—I had to wear them to gym class. When I debuted them in line, I angled my feet in a terrible attempt at deception. From the corner of my eye, I could see classmates cocking their heads sideways trying to figure out what was going on with my shoes.

The instructor noticed something odd, but after ticking off her roll call she let me proceed for the day. I clopped around in class like a lame horse, trying my best not to trip, but it was a pathetic scene. The teacher sent me home with a note: "Your daughter needs tennis shoes for gym class." With authority stepping in, I had new shoes before the week was out.

Gilbert Gets Weird

"How does it feel to know you have *24 hours to live?*" That's what the note said— the note written by Gilbert and left on the door of a lady who lived on our street. We didn't know the lady and she didn't know us, but the childish lettering quickly led police to the culprit—the poor kid next door. Gilbert got off with a warning and the lady escaped with her life, but the incident exposed the troubling thoughts inside the head of Roy's first-born son.

Mom Strengthens

Church attendance couldn't go by the wayside so mom quickly settled us at Bethany Chapel, home of the mighty prophet David Schoch. Despite his failed prophesy over dad in Spearfish (and failed resurrection on the day he died), mom considered their history good. Since our cousins also attended, it was a natural fit for our family.

Mom soon got to know a couple big shots at Bethany Chapel: Jack & Clara Gardner. Though the Gardners thumped their bibles hard, they were kind to mom and helped her restart life in the Pentecostal world. The Gardners set mom up with a part-time job in the church office and, more importantly, fixed her dental problems: Mom needed top and bottom partial bridges to replace her decayed teeth, and the Gardners paid to have it done—a huge boost to the self-esteem of a 35-year-old widow.

Besides physical repair, the Gardner's also provided spiritual repair by making mom a Sunday School teacher and installing her on the organ for Sunday service.

Bethany Chapel was a popular church whose congregation consisted of sophisticated city dwellers—not the hayseeds mom was used to. Placing her on the organ (and entrusting her with the children) was a perfect confidence-restoring move by the Gardners—one they'd come to regret.

* * *

With 1957 in the bag and 1958 quickly moving forward, Elsie stands up straight again. Now receiving generous social security payments, she uses that money to rent a house on St Louis Avenue, one block away from Bethany Chapel. Her new teeth means she no longer hides her smile, and Elsie has a pretty one—she even goes blonde to complete the look. She's still medicated, but for the first time in her life, Elsie becomes her own person.

A new day rises on Elsie Rasmussen; Life's garden looks rosy and bright. Nobody sees the terrible weed growing beneath her feet.

Church Questions

Mom clamped down hard to keep the house running smooth—as a single parent to teenage daughters, a troublesome son, and another one on her hand, she had no choice. She even invited a piggish Brazilian exchange-missionary named Glenda to live with us as a temporary overseer. Glenda had hairy arms, rampant acne, and boils on her armpits that she squeezed until they erupted; She was an intimidating presence, and in these very early days, mom's method to keep us under control. If we showed mom we could behave, she'd do away with Glenda. If not, Glenda would stay indefinitely.

Mom's strictest rule was that we had to be at church anytime the doors were open, which meant six days a week. There was no after-school fun with friends for us; If we weren't at school then we had to be at church—period. I followed her church rule, but mom soon grew unhappy with my behavior there—specifically the behavior of my mouth.

Church people always confused me because they never asked the obvious questions. Now older and bolder, I asked those questions at Bethany Chapel, but nobody ever answered me—they just shrugged their shoulders and walked away. My pointed questions in Sunday School, things like, "Why does Jesus let bad things happen to children if he loves them?" caused big waves in an otherwise calm pond. It wasn't long before word got around Bethany Chapel that I was making trouble, requiring mom to step in.

Mom points her gun-fingers at me: Thumb up, index finger held straight to form a long pointed barrel. She's got me pegged right between the eyes.

"Knock it off, Janice," mom says sternly.

I play dumb. "Knock what off?"

"Your questions. Stop questioning people in church!"

"Why can't I ask questio—"

"Knock it off right now! Knock it off!"

And that was that. There was no reasoning behind it, just a stern command that I had to obey unless I wanted to suffer mom's terrible wrath (and more Glenda). I still asked questions—I just kept them in my head. In retrospect that was a good thing, because if anyone's wrath was worse than mom's, it was that of Bethany Chapel's pastor: The Mighty David Schoch.

David Schoch: The Breath Mint Prophet

Take 140 pounds of thick torso, screw an angry head on top, then pop a mint in its mouth. Congratulations—you've just constructed one David Schoch.

Unlikeable and angry, David Schoch was the kind of man who laughed at others' expense and surrounded himself with those who did the same. He was slightly famous in the oddball world of Pentecostalism, having fashioned himself a tough talker with the magical skill of prophecy—fortune telling without a crystal ball. Stretched to full length, he measured only five-foot-six, but Schoch wielded his powerful voice as a weapon against larger men in the church who, in the normal world, would just as soon kick his ass. David Schoch's attitude could never work at a normal job, but it flourished within the walls of a Pentecostal church. In church he was God—and not a nice one.

Prophet Schoch made a habit out of yelling at his congregation, rebuking them on a weekly basis for sins both real and imagined. Attendance was mandatory at Bethany Chapel since a no-show meant missed tithes and offerings—if you're dying, give us a call and we'll add you to the prayer list, otherwise stop sinning and get your ass in church. To David Schoch, the congregation were idiot sheep that he was forced to shepherd. He was *half* right.

David Schoch's wife was Annabel, a serious woman who managed the church's sinful youth. During service, teenagers and young adults were herded into a roped-off

David Schoch with wife Annabel. This man was a real-life prophet!

area on the left side of the church, the same side where Annabel sat on stage. Ushers controlled access to the area and inspected for gum chewers and chit-chatters. Bathroom breaks weren't allowed—once you entered the pen, you stayed there until service was over.

From her chair, Annabel sat in profile to the youth group, one ear perked for any ungodly noises coming from the herd. A whispered voice, a passed paper, even a growling stomach was met with Annabel's angry gaze. If Annabel wanted discipline, she gestured to head usher Brother Toppin who then raced up the aisle to issue us a stern warning. More serious disturbances—a giggle or a yawn—brought the Prophet's wrath: David Schoch would halt the sermon, point his finger at our group, and issue a powerful rebuke that rattled the stained-glass windows and everyone's nerves. When that happened, nobody dared breathe.

Like her Prophet husband, Annabel also claimed divine messaging. In the thrilling moments when song worship concluded—that time before the sermon when voices and organ chords combined to summon the Holy Spirit—Annabel came forth with spontaneous new songs for the church to sing (first signaling to the organist what key to play). Annabel sang her simple melodies as the organ tracked her and the congregation hummed along in dim-witted bliss. When Annabel was finished, Prophet Schoch instructed the congregation to hum her new songs throughout the week so they could be learned and sung properly at future services.

When Annabel's sheep eventually sang those precious songs back to her, she must have exploded inside.

David & Annabel Schoch kept their flock obedient, but they couldn't alter history, and the Prophet now had an annoying problem he couldn't escape: the Rasmussen widow. David Schoch's tongue placed a heavy bet on Roy Rasmussen years ago, predicting that the young evangelist would travel far and wide spreading the Gospel. It was a slam-dunk guess, *except that it wasn't.* In the case of Roy—who received that prophecy from David Schoch before up and dying a few years later—it was a false prophecy that needed forgetting. So too must Schoch's failed healing of Roy be forgotten. Unfortunately, Roy's attractive young widow now occupied Bethany Chapel's center square—the church organ—and she played it like nobody's business. With four young children in tow, even the mighty David Schoch would be hard pressed to override respected church members like the Gardners, who placed her on the organ and mobilized others to donate to the needy Christian widow. As much as he'd love to bus the whole miserable lot back to Detroit, David Schoch was instead forced to suck on the lowly Rasmussens like a shit-flavored breath mint. The challenge to his ego was infuriating.

BETHANY CHAPEL

Bethany Chapel became (and remained) a living, breathing character in our lives from the 1950s up through the 1990s. It's only fair to readers that I further elaborate on what Bethany Chapel was—and what happened inside of it—so its impact on us can be better understood.

Bible School & Other Gimmicks

At Bethany Chapel, pastors and staff actively discouraged their youth from attending state colleges, instead promoting so-called "Bible Schools" or "Bible Colleges" for higher education. Pentecostal staff taught that attending secular college resulted in spiritual corruption; They went to great lengths explaining what that meant, but the simple answer was that they'd lose control of young people who tasted freedom (and rational thought) at a real college. That loss would then ripple back on the church, who'd end up with less young, fertile couples carrying the Pentecostal torch of worldly denial into the future. Without growth, the church would ultimately find itself filled with elderly dinosaurs on social security. Then it would die.

Occasionally, students defied church advice and attended state college. Upon revisiting the church, any sign of secular thought from them resulted in church members—including friends—shunning the now-corrupt *bad apples* who'd become tools of the Devil. The cold-shoulder treatment eventually caused the bad apples to leave before they could *spoil the bunch,* but the best approach was always prevention: divert them to Bible School and you'd never have an issue.

Much less serious were the endless gimmicks used to keep us entertained through the years. *Laughing in the Spirit* was one of those. This occurred at the end of song service when the congregation droned and hummed together to conjure the Holy Spirit. An instigator would suddenly fire off a high-pitched laugh, others followed, and soon the whole church was holding their sides and guffawing. During this mass hysteria, I'd scope out the biggest weirdos in the group—the adults whose laughter was *a little too intense* compared to others. The Pastor's official line was that these laughter fits were the spirit of God working through you—I thought it was just gas.

More mundane was when church leadership apparently got their hands on a *National Geographic* and co-opted the idea of praying to the four corners of the world. This short-lived directive confused the congregation, most of whom thought *north* was always the direction they were facing at any given moment. After some basic instruction, leadership succeeded in getting everyone on the same page. They all turned together, chanted and prayed, then turned again until the compass was complete. From the church balcony it looked like line dancing.

By far, the worst of the gimmicks was the foot-washing service. It happened only once a year—just enough time for church pigs to grow their feet nice and ripe for the creeps burning with a desire to touch them.

At the foot-washing service, churchgoers would jot down the names of people they disliked, approach them with white *redemption* cloths, and offer to wash that person's hooves in a bowl of water. If their offer was accepted, these weirdos got to undress that person's feet and dunk them in their bowl. Then they'd scrub the victim's soles while begging forgiveness for their ill feelings and—let's be honest here—the erections they had while molesting feet. Every year, I'd spot narrow-eyed church weirdos eyeing me from afar, redemption cloths in hand—all dying to get at my feet. I'd flee up to the balcony and stay there.

Like a failing appetizer on a dinner menu, these gimmicks were only popular with a small crowd and eventually disappeared, but Bethany Chapel didn't make it's reputation on appetizers: The big draw at Bethany Chapel was the main course—Presbytery.

The Week of Presbytery

The biggest event at Bethany Chapel—bigger than Christmas, bigger than Easter—was when Latter Rain's hottest prophets flew in from around the world for the week-long charade known as Presbytery. Bethany Chapel was a missionary church—the kind that sends volunteers off to foreign lands to spread the word of Jesus. Presbytery was the event where those missionaries were chosen.

In the year building up to Presbytery, Bethany's most-adventurous couples submitted missionary applications to David Schoch. Applicants were financially and spiritually vetted, and when Presbytery finally arrived, those who remained faced the final hurdle—a physical test in the form of a five-day fast. At the end of it all, Presbytery's esteemed panel of prophets crowned the winning couples, awarding them two-year trips to third-world countries where they'd live rough while sowing the seeds of Pentecost.

To people on the outside—applicants and viewers—this was all divine intervention. The applicants applied and—through spontaneous prophesies delivered by one or more of the prophets—Jesus chose some couples and passed on others. These people supposedly had no knowledge of whether they'd be accepted as missionaries, and if they were accepted, no knowledge of where in the world they'd be sent.

While the couples might have been too naive to figure things out—or too faithful to question it—the prophets obviously coordinated ahead of time and had full confidence in their selections. The church as a business knows where it wants to go, so if the broader network wants to prospect in Caracas, they float the idea around and wait for a dipshit couple to express interest. With a full year of church gossip before Presbytery, potential destinations are leaked and reactions gauged to avoid disastrous false prophesies. For instance, if a couple were blindsided by a prophecy sending them to Japan, but the husband declines because he's *allergic to fish,* the prophecy would be exposed as fake and the whole charade would crumble. There was always some sort of buy-in from the couples—even if informal or unwitting. And without a doubt, the most-connected couples got to choose their mission far in advance of the big day.

That isn't to say it wasn't exciting, because it was. The stakes were high—with two years away in the mission field, couples awarded missionary status had to quit their jobs, relying instead on a modest church stipend plus any handouts received from their new indigenous friends. Sometimes the couples mission was to relieve a returning missionary—like a wrestling tag-in. The fresh couple—excited to enter the ring and really *strut their stuff*—soon learned the harsh reality of missionary work from their exhausted counterparts, who'd spent the last two years begging God for the chance to sleep in a bed without a mosquito net.

Missionary selection also offered the element of chance, courtesy of the five-day fast. The only food allowed for applicants was red Jello—used to signify the coagulated blood of Jesus. Water was okay of course, but sex was absolutely prohibited. This was all considered a test of faith, though in reality it allowed the church to see who would crack when the inevitable *what the hell do I eat in this strange country* question arose upon landing in the third world—if a couple can't last a week on good ol' American Jello, the church ain't approving them for two years away in no-man's-land eating *god knows what.*

For those of us observing from the pews, the event was spellbinding—like a Church Olympics. It was a multi-night affair, beginning on Tuesday and ending on Sunday. Each night, the prophets kicked off the show by calling out the names of prospect couples. Those couples quietly rose from their seats at the rear, obediently making their way to the front where the prophets sat in judgment. Upon reaching the stage, couples were given the option to kneel or prostrate themselves as the prophets prayed over them and divine prophecies sprang forth. The prophets—colorful, well dressed, and engaging—made a show of it, with big flourishes of arms and handkerchiefs.

The first night was always easy, but once the third night came around you'd see prospects wilting on their starvation diet of red jello. They grew weaker by the hour, and come Saturday night you'd watch them using canes or even walkers to make their way up to the belly-full prophets. A few show-offs refused the helpful arms of ushers who tried escorting them—they wanted to show the prophets how strong they were by wobbling up the aisle like babies learning to walk. The worst of the bunch—the pale, shaky ones haunted by red jello nightmares—got a cracker in the mouth and orange juice on the tongue. By this time, nobody kneeled in front the prophets, electing instead to prostrate themselves—to lie down and take a load off. I always wanted to giggle, but the silence rule was in effect for the crowd —if you weren't praying, you stayed quiet. God was in the room—this was a big deal.

On the final night of Presbytery, a giant meal was prepared and served to the prophets by women in the church. These women were officially called servants, and it was considered a great honor to be a servant to these men. Final tithes and offerings were also taken for the prophets—one can only imagine how much they earned during their Southern California vacation.

For all the hype behind Bethany Chapel's big yearly Presbytery, in reality it was just one big circle jerk. Each prophet's appearance boosted the others' reputations, including the reputation of Prophet David Schoch. The excitement of the *Church Olympics* inspired new goobers to give it a shot the following year, when the same prophets arrived—fatter and richer—to repeat the cycle.

It wouldn't be long before one of our very own found themselves kneeling before the prophets.

St Louis Avenue

The St Louis house where we now lived had a second-story addition that was only accessible by outside stairs. It had no plumbing or heating, but it became a shared bedroom for me and Lana and I loved it. Our private bedroom was the first time since dad died that I could spend time together with my big sister.

I discovered that Lana wasn't as scary as I'd once believed. She was quiet and humorless—never telling a joke and never laughing at one—but very cool and clever. Lana valued rules and organization—it's no surprise that she liked spending time at church with her rule-following cousins.

Lana was also completely boy crazy. Naturally pretty and curvy, she presented a challenge to the boys at church and knew exactly how to play them. Even the hand-me-down clothes she wore looked sharp. My big sister became my idol— someone that I looked up to and wanted to emulate. Unfortunately, that idol looked down on me. Who could blame her?

After a year or so of mom holding steady in Long Beach, Lyle Lenning invited her to apply at the Post Office where he worked. It was rare in those days for women to work a man's job but Lyle knew the church office gig was a dead end for her —she was capable of far better. Mom wasn't worldly but she was smart—much smarter than dad—and when Lyle got her a seat at the Post Office's twice-a-year written test, she passed it with flying colors. Her Post Office career began in 1959, when she started throwing mail on the graveyard shift.

Throwing mail was exactly how it sounded and mom practiced it regularly, setting up cardboard cubbyholes at home and hurling sample mail into the appropriate cubby (separated by zip code). She'd arrive home from work at 6am, sleep on the couch, then continue honing her throwing skill before work.

> Fearful of losing her opportunity at the Post Office, Elsie's main focus shifts from church to work. Her overnight work hours cause repeat tardiness at church, and the elders take note. She's still the organist and still a Sunday School teacher, but Elsie's empowering herself through real work and the church knows they're losing control of her. If she doesn't tighten up her Christianity, there'll be hell to pay.

Around this time, Lana started giving tryouts to the boys in town. To create the illusion of holiness, the boys either came from church or were brought there by Lana, but once they came back to our house, all bets were off. Lana and her boy-of-the-month would hide under the outside stairs for private make-out sessions, then cuddle on the steps and makeout some more. I often stepped over their writhing bodies while ascending the stairs to our bedroom.

Mom was mostly absent in the evenings—her whereabouts a mystery described simply as "work"—but she was aware of the boys and now strong enough to dismiss them over Lana's pleas. Mom's rationale for disliking a boy could be anything: Blonde Jerry Ashmore was a sneak—evidenced by the disrespectful way he chewed gum. Trent Wood—an Elvis lookalike from a church family—was a phony and a troublemaker. Once mom disapproved of a boy, Lana was forced to break off the romance. She cried many tears for them, especially for handsome Trent Wood— I mean he looked *just like Elvis*.

Lana recovered quickly from these disposable boys though, and for good reason: Her sights were set on the biggest fish in Bethany Chapel's small pond—and he still swam free.

The Swinging Shepherds

Bryl-creemed hair: check. Two-tone spats: check. Pinky ring: check. *Virgin:* check. These were the young men of Bethany Chapel who called themselves the Swinging Shepherds. Equal parts car club and bible study, the Shepherds cruised downtown Long Beach looking to score souls for Christ while scoping out tits along the way. They were all sanctified virgins—a church term describing proudly virginal men who kept themselves pure for a future wife. Everyone else called them nerds. The Shepherds' leader was Dave Copp, an affable young man in his early twenties who looked the part in his pin-striped suit and gold-cross cufflinks. He was Bethany Chapel's big fish—the one all the church girls wanted—and his mother knew it.

If ever a name did not fit a person, that name was *Rose* Copp. Rose was Bethany's other widow, but in contrast to Elsie Rasmussen, Rose was filled to the brim with money and arrogance. Devoutly Christian and perpetually crabby, Rose aspired towards leadership in the church world, but that dream died with her husband, air-traffic controller James Copp. Everyone liked James, but Rose killed the buzz in every room she entered because she postured herself like the Queen of England. Rose subscribed to the snobbish church idea that poor people sinned more often than rich people, thus requiring her to elevate her head to avoid the sinful stench emanating from Christianity's *lower rung*.

Rose's two sons, John & Dave, were her jewels, and she'd not let them go to anyone below their status. A completely fair rule, but one the cold-hearted Rose didn't understand could be turned on its head by a human emotion called *love*.

Enter one Lana Rasmussen. She'd known for years that our family was a lost cause, and with high school graduation just around the corner, Lana's exit plan was coming due. She already ran through all the boys, even giving John Copp a tryout—they all whiffed. Now the Swingingest Shepherd of all was up to bat, and Lana lobbed him the slowest, fattest pitch she could possibly throw. A blind man could hit it, but Dave wasn't blind, in fact he saw it all very clearly. Dave was in love and Lana was too—together they hit a home run.

Rose was extremely upset. The Copps were big shots at Bethany Chapel, a family without sin whose money held much sway with church leadership. Dave could have picked any established girl he wanted—even those from other churches—but he settled on one who was seven years younger, the daughter of a dead preacher, now raised by a poor widow who worked the Post Office's graveyard shift. Word of the relationship traveled fast through the church. *The boat was rocking.*

Widow Rising from the Ashes

As it turned out, Lana wasn't the only Rasmussen woman in a relationship. Elsie was in one too, and it wasn't a good one.

Andy Taylor was Bethany Chapel's handsome trombone player. With the band and the organ seated at opposite ends of the church's stage, Andy was afforded unlimited flirtation with the pretty new organist, Elsie Rasmussen—and once all flirtation was spent, he'd stand up and play his big trombone.

Andy worked at Douglas Aircraft and also owned a donut shop. His brother Orvel was the wealthy pastor of nearby Colonial Tabernacle, a progressive church whose congregants were all going to hell in David Schoch's eyes, but hey—horn players are hard to find.

Besides the oddity of Andy Taylor coming from a competing church, there was a far bigger problem: Andy Taylor was married. With two children. Who sat in the front row at Bethany Chapel.

How and when the affair began is unknown, but we'd only been back to Long Beach for a year or so at this time. Lana—being the oldest—may have picked up on it, but the rest of us were too young to recognize anything amiss. In retrospect, mom's evening absences make a lot more sense when considering a secret social life with Andy Taylor. We knew mom took the bus to work at night, but how did she get home? And why did she often bring donuts?

Their affair was as reckless as one could be, but Andy's worldly charm was light years beyond Elsie's experience with Roy, the hayseed preacher with rubberbanded shirt sleeves snapped 'round his forearms. To a simple widow from Bruce, the experience of being entertained by a city man five years younger, combined with

About 24. 25 years there were 5 Rasmussen's living here in LB ~~and~~ who were as poor as possible.

Lyle Fenning said to me why don't you try get a job with the Post Office. At that time the P.O had not hired women since during World War II — But The Lord opened the door for me to get a job with the P.O.

Fran K

Mom's description of us in Long Beach: "...as poor as possible."

empowerment through work, went straight to her head. Elsie floated in the clouds —life be damned.

Breath Mint Prophet Goes 0-2

God granted David Schoch another opportunity to save a life with his magic hands —the life of his wife Annabel, who'd suffered a major illness and was clinging to life. The church's *Prayer Warriors* held nightly vigils over a week's time—I attended and broke Annabel's gum-chewing rule to spite her—but Jesus eventually got her in the end. When the mighty David Schoch announced her passing at Sunday service, I studied his eyes to see if they shed tears. Not a drop.

It wasn't long before the Prophet fancied another bride, a pretty Texan named Audene. Audene's husband, Pastor Flowers, had recently flown his plane into the *non-sand* part of the desert floor, leaving her widowed with a young child. Prophet Schoch was well acquainted with Pastor Flowers and Audene, having been the keynote speaker at several of their Texas camp meetings over the years. Replacing unattractive Annabel with the charming Audene would be a huge *man win* for David Schoch; likewise, scoring a prophet would be a catapult-shot into the higher echelons of Christian society for Audene. The only thing needed was some wife polishing, courtesy of the private women's retreats that teach pastors' wives how to conduct themselves while their husbands scream and yell from the pulpit.

Audene Schoch's debut was a big hit at Bethany Chapel, where her natural charm and poise quickly caused everyone to forget about Annabel. Whereas Annabel was a take-charge minister with ego and drive, Audene was simply a pleasant woman who supported her husband while he did the dirty work. The youth group in particular loved Audene—we no longer had to suffer under Annabel's angry glare. If one of us locked eyes with Audene, the only thing she returned was a smile.

Trauma Shows Itself

The trauma of the last few years began showing itself in odd ways. Gilbert, then eleven years old, wasn't growing and we seriously thought he might be a dwarf. Mark was five but rarely spoke. And I, at thirteen years old, suddenly developed extremely large breasts. Mom (and dad) never took us to a doctor for anything— not for the unbearable ear aches I'd get in South Dakota, not for the funk rashes we'd get at the farmhouse—but mom took me in for my breasts. She had no choice really, since they caused a scene every time I went out in public with Gilbert (my constant sidekick). Strangers pointed and laughed at my breasts; We laughed too because they were so ridiculous. The sight of us walking down the street—he too short and me too chesty—was an odd pairing indeed.

The doctor confirmed that my abnormal breasts were the result of dad dying just as I hit puberty, and assured me that they'd return to normal size in a year or so. I felt better about the situation and hoped time would pass quickly. My horny boy cousins, however, wanted time to stop.

Cousins Wrestle My Breasts

With mom always away at night, the after-dark rule of the house was that we had to be at church or at home, nowhere else. Since mom now received social security payments plus a paycheck from work, food was no longer an issue for us. Smelling free food, our nearby cousins frequently showed up to eat with us. Once everyone was finished and burping out their meals, it was time to wrestle.

Wrestling matches began with jokes and laughter, but it always ended the same way —one of the cousins would grab me and we'd tumble to the floor. I'd be pinched all over and giggle, then we'd stand up and another cousin would have a turn. It was like a football game where I was the football. I had no idea why they liked wrestling me so much, but I loved the attention and if they were copping a feel, so be it. It was our entertainment and I enjoyed seeing my brothers laugh.

* * *

Church Hounds

While inspecting my face for acne one Sunday morning, I hear the urgent voice of Sister Lou Winans coming from the ground floor where mom and the boys sleep. A gangly busybody with a cursed complexion, Sister Winans was part of the *in* crowd at Bethany Chapel. The woman was sure to be sour any time of day, and today it was 8am—which meant mom was still asleep from her overnight work shift. I head downstairs to see what the fuss is about.

"Wake up, Sister Elsie!"

I enter the living room and see mom struggling to rise from the couch. Sister Winans leans over her.

"Sister Elsie, you have Sunday School and the organ today! Get dressed and get to church!"

Gilbert watches from the front door he'd opened for Sister Winans when she knocked—giving her enough room to barge in and head straight for mom. This wasn't the first time church people had invaded our space—they'd also done so at the failed healing of my dying father. Now they're harassing the only parent I have left, waking her up to demand she perform her volunteer duties at church.

"Sister Elsie, stop your sinning!"

"What's going on?" I interrupt.

Surprised by my sudden presence, Sister Winans' tone instantly softens. "Dear, your mom's been on my heart all week! Jesus told me to drop in and check on her."

"Don't call me dear, you gross windbag," my internal voice replies. I hated all the church people by now and hoped they knew it.

Sister Winans reads my thoughts—she knows I caught her in a bad light. She changes face, gently returning her attention to mom.

"You know how much we all care for you, Sister Elsie. We want you to stay strong with the Lord!"

More crap from her mouth. I'd recently learned to make the *devil's curse* with my fingers, and I deployed it at her—behind my back.

Mom breaks the tension with an apology, stumbling to the bathroom to change from her nightgown as Sister Winans slinks out the door. I was disappointed with mom: Rather than standing up to Sister Winans with a firm, "I can't make it today because I just came home from work at 6am, now *get out of my house and don't ever come back,*" mom simply rolled over and gave in.

Bethany Chapel's leaders learned something important about Elsie Rasmussen that day: She submits to church authority no matter how obnoxious it is. A precedent was set.

* * *

We had another surprise visitor the following Sunday afternoon: David Schoch, head pastor of Bethany Chapel. Even though we lived only a short block from church, the great Prophet's *Christian heart* had never before directed him to visit the church *widow*—this was his first time in our home.

I answered the knock on our door since mom was busy preparing for her overnight shift. I was surprised to see Prophet Schoch, since we'd just seen him a few hours ago at service. After the most basic of hellos, he entered our home and began pacing the floor.

Me and the boys watched David Schoch stomp around in our living room like a bull before the charge, breath steaming out a mixture of coffee and artificial mint. Mom stopped what she was doing, taking a seat in the living room as the Prophet paced. We all waited for him to speak—and knew it would be bad when he did.

"Elsie Rasmussen! You'll stop this behavior right now!"

The Prophet sticks a finger in mom's face. She allows it.

"I rebuke you and your sinning, Elsie Rasmussen! You'll stop it now, or else!"

The sin these church people kept mentioning was still a great mystery to us kids. We'd never met Andy Taylor and knew nothing about him. All we knew was the action unfolding in our living room: Bethany Chapel's head honcho pointing a finger in mom's face and rebuking her—the church world's strongest possible scolding. Behind my back, ten fingers once again curled into the *devil's curse.*

Mom, of course, knew what was really going on. During Sister Winans recent intrusion into our home, mom never asked what her sin was, she just sat there and took everything Sister Winans dished out. The same occurred with the Prophet, who now stood in mom's face unloading his powerful voice at full blast.

The Prophet continued his high-amplitude tirade; The walls shook and our ears bled. Mom cried under the Prophet's rebuke. His manner was so threatening that I thought he would hit her, and I was ready to attack if he did. Then, as suddenly as it began, it ended—David Schoch took a deep breath of his own hot air and exited our home, leaving us in deafening silence. The only evidence he'd appeared at all was the stale minty aroma left behind.

I noticed something interesting about mom during the ordeal: Though she cried throughout, it was a different cry from the one she had for dad. That cry was tragic, with his death leaving her emotionally collapsed for months. Prophet Schoch's tirade, however, elicited crying without emotion. Within seconds of him leaving, mom was back up and preparing for work as if nothing happened. We thought she was in deep trouble—I mean, this man was a *Prophet*—but she didn't seem fazed and never said a word to us about it. Mom didn't care.

I never liked David Schoch, and now I liked him even less. Bethany Chapel's mighty *Prophet of God* exposed his true self by entering a widow's home—his first and only visit—to berate her in front of her children. The Bible says many things about widows—none of them are *that.* Did Prophet Schoch ask us how we were doing? Did he give an encouraging talk to the fatherless boys? *And how is school, Janice?* Nope. The only thing David Schoch brought to the widow's children was a foul mouth spewing venom at their mom. And the worst was yet to come.

The Two-Headed Snake

It was obvious that someone inside the church was spying on mom & Andy's affair, and the suspect list was long. Andy's wife (seated in the first row) ranked high on the list, as did local Rasmussen relatives who never liked mom. Rose Copp had motive, too: her prized son Dave was now engaged to Lana and she desperately wanted to tank the marriage. Whoever the spy was, their updates filled the gossip tanks of empty old church ladies who exchanged rumors and half-truths every Sunday in defiance of the biblical teachings they conveniently ignored. These bitter women were elated to learn the affair didn't end—in fact it was only beginning.

Since Elsie proved such a hard nut to crack, the church went for the softest target of all: her kids. Roy's cousin, Bethany Chapel man George Sterud, concocted a plan with Albin Rasmussen to ambush Elsie's children after school while she was away at work. Albin never attended Bethany Chapel, but that didn't matter—this was personal.

Even though both men live on our street, they still bring a car—idling it in front of our house, windows down, with George sitting shotgun. Albin appears at our front door, informing me and Lana that he needs to speak with us in the car. Alarm bells immediately trigger in my head —the last time Albin spoke to me in a car, he told me dad was dead. Was he gonna tell me mom died too?

I'm in tears before we even reach the car. Lana is not. We slide into the backseat with Albin now in the driver's seat. He and George turn around to unload on us.

"Your mom is a very bad person!" Albin yells.

"If these were bible days," George threatens, "She'd be stoned on the public square for what she's doing!"

The men never explain to us what mom is doing, but I sense it has to do with the bad word: sex. As I cry next to an emotionless Lana, the men nod each other on, sternly repeating that our mom is a very bad person.

Gilbert rounds the corner of our street from whatever trouble he's been up to; he sees me crying in the car with Albin & George, two men making a big show of things with waved arms and yelling. Gilbert hears the word mom and jumps to the same conclusion as me: *She's dead.* Panicked, he runs into the house and calls her at work.

"Albin says there's something wrong with you!" Gilbert blurts through tears.

Mom reassures Gilbert that she's alright, ends the call, then promptly faints off her work stool. She's sent home from work, but before she arrives to stop the men, George Sterud sinks his fangs into Gilbert, too—he walks Gilbert down to his home where he repeats the same venom: "Your mom is a very bad person! She should be stoned!"

* * *

More time passed as the dutiful church spies watched for the affair to end. Andy and his trombone vanished from Bethany Chapel, leaving his wife & children to soldier on. Elsie was relieved of her volunteer duties on the organ, though she continued paying tithes and attending services whenever she wasn't working. After hitting Elsie directly—then going after her children—there wasn't much more the church could do short of throwing her out. Complicating things to the point of absurdity was the church's announcement of a big-time wedding: That of Dave Copp to Lana Rasmussen.

Wedding Plans

Dave Copp was a virgin, and nobody was happier about it than his humorless mother Rose. Now, the virginity she'd worked so hard to preserve was being awarded to Lana Rasmussen, daughter of the poor (and adulterous) widow Elsie Rasmussen—a fact that made Rose want to set her head on fire. She'd policed the young couple hard, insisting they could never be alone in a room together, though that was unnecessary since Lana was also proud of their virginities. The two were sanctified virgins who'd meet each other's privates for the very first time after marriage and hope for no *unpleasant surprises.*

Like Rose, mom was also opposed to the marriage, insisting to Lana that Dave was out of her class and she should choose a lesser man. Though both mothers' agreed on the lower-class status of the Rasmussens, this mattered little to the young couple who wanted each other's privates come hell or high water.

Mom was absent from Lana's wedding plans (claiming she was too busy with work), but as maid of honor I helped her prepare and enjoyed the normal conversations we had together: Lana complained about Rose, describing petty things the old crow did to show her who the real boss was. Lana told me how mom pleaded with her not to marry Dave, since he was so far out of her class. Unsolicited, Lana divulged to me that she and Dave were virgins—perhaps wanting to set an example for her fourteen-year old sister who was on the verge of being wild. These were the only honest conversations I'd ever had with with my big sister and I wanted more, but I knew they would end once November 20, 1959 rolled around —on that day, privates would be exposed.

A Public Stoning

The wedding day arrived and went off without a hitch. The newlywed Copps were now ascending royalty within Bethany Chapel: Dave's mother was God's

Groom Dave Copp flanked by the Swinging Shepherds

most loyal woman, and Lana's father was a preacher who died serving the Lord. But what to do about Lana's mother, the adulterous widow? That question was answered a few weeks later—just in time for Christmas.

Somewhere along the way, church leaders convinced mom that the only way back from her sin was to attend a special Sunday evening forgiveness service featuring her as the main event. Perhaps she was forced to sacrifice herself for Lana's greater good; Perhaps she just accepted a terrible deal. Whatever the negotiations, Gilbert and I were in the dark about it. We simply showed up to church one evening, surprised to see a packed crowd. When Prophet Schoch called mom up to the pulpit, I thought she was going to win an award until I realized nobody was clapping.

Bethany Chapel's sanctuary is silent as sin—no words, all eyes—as the nervous, pale widow walks toward the stage. It's a dreadful walk—the march of a woman about to be stoned. She reaches the base of the stage and her foot suddenly catches in the carpet—she stumbles but collects herself. Mounting the stage, the widow turns around for the congregation to see her face. To see her tears.

"I have sinned before God and the church," she meekly admits. Elsie coughs and mumbles further repentances, begging the chapel's forgiveness. Her daughter Janice, seated in the pews, can't believe what she's seeing—her mother standing alone on stage to get beat up by strangers.

After many long minutes, the widow finishes her repentance. The church sits amazed at the display of humility put on by the mighty David Schoch. Eyes fill with tears—not for the humiliated widow, but for Jesus' tender mercies. Hearty applause turns to rejoicing that it's all over now—the adulterous widow is cleansed of her sin.

David Schoch—the egomaniac who called himself a Prophet—entered a widow's home to yell at her in front of her children. He forced that widow to humiliate herself in front of his congregation. Seems the person begging forgiveness should have been *him.*

In the end, church leadership wanted blood and they got blood. Though Jesus *theoretically* had forgiven mom for her sins, had anyone in the church forgiven her? The entire purpose of mom's gross public humiliation was to stain her—not forgive her—and that mission was now accomplished. From that moment on, the congregation of Bethany Chapel would know the sins of Elsie Rasmussen. She was finished.

* * *

It took a few weeks before we found a new place to live. We still attended Bethany Chapel during that time—all of us except mom, who didn't return after that night. These were awkward times for outcast kids. The Jesus of the Bible would have swept us up to his bosom, but the angry Pentecostal arms of Bethany Chapel held tightly unto themselves, so we kept our heads down like prisoners close to their release date. Mom finally secured an apartment at 1453 Walnut Ave, far enough from Bethany for us to be left alone. It was also conveniently located within walking distance of our new church, Colonial Tabernacle.

COLONIAL TABERNACLE

Though still Pentecostal, the friendly leadership of Colonial Tabernacle were a world away from the everyone-goes-to-hell-but-us mentality of Bethany Chapel. A big reason for that was because Colonial Tabernacle operated under the FourSquare church organization, whereas Bethany Chapel was an independent church without oversight. If David Schoch believed the best way to run his business was by visiting widows in their homes to scream at them in front of their children, then that was that. His aggressive style was reflected in the congregation—all the angry men and women who rejoiced when a widow was humiliated for their pleasure. That could never happen at Colonial Tabernacle because FourSquare wouldn't allow it.

Colonial Tabernacle's friendly country-style atmosphere stood in stark contrast to the tension and fear we constantly felt at Bethany. Colonial had a robe-wearing choir that sang to great music, plus programs for the youth like church camp and high-school graduation celebrations. The rules were relaxed too, specifically the makeup rule: girls could wear it as long as they weren't in the choir.

Colonial's pastor was Orvel Taylor, younger brother of Andy Taylor—the other half of mom's affair. Orvel and his wife Sister Taylor could have poisoned the well for us right from the start, but they didn't. The congregation at Colonial knew nothing about our dad dying, or mom's affair with the pastor's brother—they only saw us as new friends walking through their unlocked door. It wasn't long before I tested that friendship.

Janice Makes a Splash

Friends were easy to make in the youth group, whose services occurred every Saturday night with Sister Taylor. Part of the youth service included *Testimony Time* where Sister Taylor encouraged us to offer personal examples of Jesus' impact our lives; After Testimony Time, we would all sing and bring the service to a pleasant close.

Sister Taylor & Brother Orvel Taylor.

One evening, Sister Taylor made her no-obligation invitation to Testimony Time: "Please stand and tell us how Jesus has touched your life."

By now I was comfortably settled in the youth group and decided to let my guard down. I really liked Sister Taylor and felt this was my chance to be honest with her and my new friends; I could finally share the sadness I felt watching my dad dying in front of me. I could tell them how it felt looking at his smiling corpse resting in a coffin. I was in friendly territory here, and the invitation was made. I raised my hand.

Sister Taylor called on me and I stood up. I looked at the youth group smiling at me—Sister Taylor was smiling too. I had everyone's attention, just like in Wichita when I had my vision. Now was my time to shine.

"I hate Jesus because he killed my dad," I announced.

The youth group wasn't sure if they heard me correctly, but my follow-up left them without doubt.

"Why didn't Jesus love me enough to heal my dad?" I blurted out. "I prayed all afternoon begging Jesus to bring him home, but he didn't. What did I do wrong?"

Words and tears tumbled out as I expressed the sadness I'd carried in my heart since March 17, 1957.

The church was pin-drop silent except for a back-row giggler. I gave no indication of stopping anytime soon—in fact I was just warming up. Sister Taylor took charge, rushing into an uptempo song to drown me out. I knew I was being cut off and probably should have been embarrassed, but I didn't care—it felt good.

* * *

Speaking of feeling good, mom was riding high in the saddle now that Bethany Chapel was off her back—she could continue her affair with Andy unopposed. The drama this would have caused at Colonial Tabernacle was easily fixed—mom just stopped going to church altogether. Elsie Rasmussen, the woman who'd spent her entire life in church, was headed completely off the rails.

Say Hello to Andy

Our move to the Walnut Ave apartment (and Colonial Tabernacle) coincided with Andy's first appearance in our home. It wasn't formal or special, he just started hanging out with us in the afternoon. He was charming and likeable, without arrogance, and the boys immediately liked him. Andy was an engineer & union rep for *McDonnell Douglas*—a man much savvier than mom, whose only life experience was having five babies with a farmer who drove her across the Midwest preaching Jesus. Andy also owned a donut shop and rental property. The pairing of the two didn't add up in my head, but Andy was polite and I had no reason to dislike him. Mom, on the other hand, was *really* starting to annoy me.

Once Andy was unveiled, whatever remained of mom's interest in our lives vanished. We were given a chore list to go with the standing rule—be at church or be at home—but there was no oversight because mom's entire world revolved around him. Mom was in *la-la-land* whenever Andy dropped in for the afternoon, incapable of anything but full attention to him. Her neglect wasn't a head-in-the-clouds moment either—she knew what she was doing because she consciously appointed me caretaker of Gilbert and Mark. At fifteen years old, I was tasked with making dinners I was never taught to make and teaching things I hadn't been taught myself. From that point on, my teenage years were no longer possible to enjoy—and it only got worse from there.

* * *

Andy Taylor

Time blurred at the Walnut Ave apartment as mom became more enraptured with Andy—her only involvement with us was saying *no* to anything we wanted to do. In my freshman year of high school, I saw the baton-twirling majorettes and decided to be one. At home I practiced my baton skills, but once mom saw it, I was out: Baton twirling was too close to dancing—mom's mortal sin along with drinking alcohol—and the case was closed. I wouldn't have time for it anyways, considering the steadily growing chore list with my name on it.

Clean Floors and White Cake

We barely saw mom during the week. We knew she went to breakfast after work with her Post Office friends (arriving back home after we left for school), but besides that we never knew where she was—which meant she was with Andy. To keep us captive, she left a daily chore list to complete after school. My list was always the longest.

Filling mom's lunch thermos with rice & corn was a simple task, no big deal for me other than the fact that she could just *do it herself.* Cleaning the kitchen and bathroom floors every week was my least favorite because she always inspected my work early in the morning, and if I failed she made me get up early on Saturday to re-clean everything. My Friday chore was bizarre—I had to bake mom a white cake with frosting, ready to eat when she came home from work. My church friends knew about it and laughed, thinking mom was just being funny—they didn't know that mom never laughed with us.

Once per month, mom had a long weekend off from work. We dreaded that weekend because mom was so difficult, turning the written chore list into a verbal one. Mom constantly harped about our laziness: *"Come on let's get going!"* she'd holler at us in the morning. We gently teased her in response, "Where are we going mother?" but that just made her mad. She didn't get the joke.

Mom forced me and Gilbert to get part-time jobs once we were old enough to work, then required us to pay rent to her and a 10% tithe to the church (which I never did). This was a woman who no longer went to church and was now three years into an affair with a married man. The hypocrisy of it made my head spin, but there was no escaping it—mom made sure we toed the line by threatening to call *Child Services* and turn us over to foster care if we didn't do as she said. It was a standing threat—repeated often—and we took it very seriously.

School Work

The part-time job I found was at a finance company in downtown Long Beach. Each day after school, I took a city bus down to Broadway Ave, then caught another bus home after dark; Since I was alone and the bus stop on Anaheim St was a few blocks away from Walnut, I walked urgently to get home and out of the dark. Once home, I'd cook some type of slop experiment for Gilbert, Mark, and me. Whatever I cooked never tasted good so we used a lot of ketchup to make it better. Sometimes I just threw in the towel and we ate ketchup sandwiches.

Gilbert got a job cleaning fast-food restaurants after they closed. We were fortunate since our earnings paid for school lunches, but young Mark was left out in the cold and had to steal money from mom's purse while she slept. Even though he only needed money for lunch, he always felt like a thief doing it. When Gilbert found out Mark had to sneak money for lunch, he stepped in and gave him money from his own pocket instead.

It seems obvious that we could just ask mom for money, but it didn't work that way in our home. Mom never sat down and asked about school or church or anything else in our lives, because she was completely uninterested in our needs. We knew that asking her for the simplest thing—something as small as a signature on a report card—would result in a big scene that ended with us punished for bothering her. We just signed them ourselves, doing everything we could to keep mom out of our business.

Bunker for One

Gilbert built a bunker for himself at our Walnut Ave apartment. It wasn't much —just a little room tucked under the outside stairs—but it was his response to the impending threat of nuclear war, and *it only had room for one*. Good luck to the rest of us, but if someone's making it out alive, it's gonna be Roy's first-born son.

Even from a young age, Gilbert knew he had to be the Rasmussen man who no longer existed. To accomplish that he put great emphasis on the *man* part—that meant bunkers, that meant death threats, and most of all, that meant fighting. Fortunately or not, Gilbert was very short for his age (until high school), so the fights came to him. When they didn't, he'd head into the streets and look for one. Many nights he'd be missing-in-action only to arrive home later with a swollen face. Even though this violated mom's *church or home* rule, we weren't concerned because she was never home to find out anyways. We knew how to work around her rules and lie when necessary to keep her satisfied—mom was always a storm waiting to descend and make our lives hell.

Copp Intervention

Somewhere along the way, the Copp newlyweds came by to speak with mom about the affair. Even though we no longer attended Bethany Chapel, they did, and Lana & Dave's ascent to the next echelon of ministry was stalled by mom's baggage. Church authorities weren't going to back the daughter of a woman who thumbed her nose at them.

The Copps invited mom to their car out front for a private conversation. Dave couldn't have known he was in over his head with mom. He was a soft soul—a man who enjoyed making others laugh at his own expense—but if Prophet Schoch couldn't make her stop, Dave Copp stood zero chance. Lana was a different story. She'd bent mom once before in taking us away from Detroit—a rewarding move that resulted in a top-tier husband. Now she needed to do it again.

I watched from the upstairs window as small talk turned to argument. Lana was very angry and yelling at mom; Dave maintained composure, opting for the polite path of reason. On and on it went, so long that I thought the car would run out of gas. Eventually, everyone talked themselves out and mom came back inside. The Copps drove away angry.

Alfred's Vacations

Another relative argued with mom around this time—her father Alfred. The man who crossed the street so many years ago to avoid meeting his grandchildren— the one who disowned his daughter and threw out Roy's gift for him—decided he wanted to reconnect now that the *river rat* was dead. For the second year in a row, Alfred arrived from South Dakota to take up space in our tiny apartment. Both of his vacations lasted from January through February—perfectly timed for the old goblin to escape Bruce's brutal winter and warm his bones in the SoCal sun. He made no contact with us between trips: no cards, no calls, no nothing. He just showed up in January masquerading as our grandpa so he could warm his purple mole.

I disliked him both times he came out. Alfred never called me by name and the only words he spoke in my direction were to boss me around, a big indicator of how he felt about women. He was nicer to the boys and they liked him—they liked any man who came around to play role model for them.

Every morning in our apartment, Alfred stewed prunes for his bowels. He explained to the boys in fine detail how his bowels functioned and why a regular diet of prunes was important to keep them free of disease. Gilbert and Mark loved hearing him ramble on about bowel health; I stuck fingers in my ears to avoid hearing about his disgusting guts.

The man took over everything, even lighting up smelly cigars in our apartment. Alfred ate our food, pooped it out with a prune, then enjoyed a nice stogie while commandeering our main source of entertainment—the television. Our friends regularly came over on Wednesday nights after church to eat potato chips and watch American Bandstand with us; Alfred put an end to it, turning his charm up to maximum rudeness to scare them away. When Alfred arrived on his SoCal vacations, we went friendless.

I frequently woke up to Alfred yelling at mom after she arrived home from work. His charge was fair—stop playing around with men and take care of your children instead—but it still pissed me off. Alfred was a nobody, a pretend grandpa who never wanted to know us and made no contact between trips. He showed up once a year expecting to be top dog, but he needed to earn our respect before demanding it. Whether his criticism of mom was accurate was beside the point: That's my mom and you're a stranger—don't yell at her.

Alfred's SoCal getaways happened over two consecutive years. On his third trip out, while overnighting with a travel buddy in separate rooms of an Arizona motel, Alfred missed his check-out time. His buddy called the room but got no answer; Notifying the manager, both men went to his motel room and opened the door—Alfred was dead. So much for the prunes.

Alfred Thompson—the man who disowned two daughters and ran across the street to avoid his grandkids—enjoys a SoCal vacation.

The Onion's Gift

Sighting Alfred Thompson at our residence, Uncle Albin must have smelled forgiveness in the air, because he too paid us a visit. Albin's appearance at the front door surprised me—though his son Paul was close with Gilbert, I hadn't seen him since the day he and George Sterud took me hostage in their car to tell me mom was a bad woman who should be stoned. I asked Albin what he needed, and he simply handed me a set of waterless cookware—the same stuff dad used to sell—telling me it was a gift for my *hope chest*; An heirloom for when I was married.

I knew Albin was a classless rube, a not-so-smart man who worked hard but had no manners. And I hadn't forgotten his long list of poor behavior—selling my dead dad's shoes and stealing his car came to mind. But I recognized that Albin's gift of cookware to sixteen-year-old me was an attempt at redemption—the best effort of a stupid man to apologize for the terrible things he said to me in the car with George. I knew I should be kinder to him, maybe even crack the door of forgiveness, but I couldn't do it. He was too wrong for too long to be forgiven.

Mark Snaps a Towel

One Wednesday night, Mark and I arrived home from church and couldn't find Gilbert. Mom's *church or home* rule had now expanded to include work, so Gilbert's absence wasn't unusual considering the odd hours he kept cleaning restaurants with older cousin Paul (including a regular gig at Park Pantry). Around 9:30pm, while we were tuned in to *I Love Lucy*, Gilbert walked in with a friend from the neighborhood named Bob Boon. Gilbert invited Mark to join them in the bedroom—the three boys entered the room and closed the door.

I thought nothing of it and continued watching television. After 15 minutes or so, I heard strange squeals and laughter coming from the boy's room. I peeked in to see what they were up to.

Lying prone on the bed was a shirtless Bob Boon, face buried in a pillow and the tips of his ears burning hot red. Big purple welts colored Bob's back—courtesy of Gilbert and Mark, who took turns snapping Bob's naked flesh with a wet towel. With each snap, Mark giggled at the highest level, in turn causing Gilbert to laugh at his little brother. Each snap also brought extreme pleasure to the red-eared Bob Boon, who moaned muffled satisfaction into his pillow. I quickly closed the door, laughing to myself at the disturbing sight.

I wasn't quite sure what I'd just witnessed, but I knew mom couldn't know since she'd only cause trouble. The best option was for Gilbert not to bring Bob around anymore, so after the boys were *finished,* I told Gilbert and he agreed. Bob Boon and his hot-red ears never returned.

Role Model

By now Andy had become a regular presence in our lives—but only on afternoons. The boys hadn't caught on to that detail but I had. Mom cried to me—her teenage confidante—complaining that Andy never took her out in public. It was obvious to me that he didn't want to be seen with her, but mom kept playing the game while making life miserable for us.

On mom's monthly weekend off from work, I'd come home from church on Sunday to see her sitting on Andy's lap, or both of them cooking burgers and having a grand old time listening to albums he gave her. Andy's favorite album was Herb

Alpert's *A Taste of Honey* because, in his words, he *really dug the cover*—that cover featured a naked woman covered in whipped cream and licking the tip of her finger. The double-standard of mom forcing us to attend church every day and follow stupid *no dancing* rules while she sinned with Andy aggravated me so much that I once slammed the front door after entering their scene. Mom immediately corrected my behavior, directing me back outside to re-enter politely for Andy.

Andy told Gilbert & Mark that he loved them and they should see him as a father figure—a nice gesture from a man who most certainly knew what he was doing. The boys needed a role model, and a suave man who played trombone and cooked burgers with mom wasn't a bad one. Andy's savvy was a great benefit to Gilbert & Mark, who'd otherwise be lost in the world of manhood. If their father figure only showed up on afternoons, so be it.

On the other hand, Andy was also a bit of a leech. If his car needed fixing or something went wrong at a rental unit, Andy would casually mention it to us, knowing that mom would gladly offer him money. He always took the money because that's how his game worked.

It would have been far better if mom had kept me out of her Andy business, but keeping private about relationship problems wasn't in her DNA—at least not with me. On those days when Andy failed to show up, mom was pathetic as she cried to me about it. Sometimes Mark and Gilbert got pulled in, too. If mom felt we weren't helping her enough with whatever her *Andy issue* was that day, she'd threaten to get drunk at a bar and run into traffic to be hit by a car. Much like her threat to call *Child Services* and make us foster kids, this wasn't a one-time threat —these threats were repeated and we took them seriously since she was the only parent we had left. We catered to every wish, doing everything we could to keep mom afloat while awaiting the magic Andy fix—once he appeared, all was better.

More Strange Noises from the Boys Room

I went home early from school one day because I didn't feel well. After entering our apartment, I heard strange noises coming from the boys' bedroom. Since it was an off-weekend for mom, I figured she must be cleaning it. I decided to investigate, knowing full well that the last time I opened the boys' door to investigate weird noises, I was greeted with the sight of Bob Boon being flogged. I apprehensively opened the door once more and peeked in. It wasn't Bob Boon on the bed this time—it was mom and Andy.

Mom was on her back with Andy above, and they were going at it like two rabbits. At sixteen, this was even more horrific than Bob Boon's flogging. Mom saw me and jumped up—butt flopping around—and beelined for the exit where I stood. She whispered *I'm so sorry* as she ran past me, never making eye contact. I didn't know what to say in the middle of this—I figured it was my fault for coming home early. In the shock of it all, I never saw Andy leave. I assume he made his exit through our second-floor window.

This was the same woman who forced me to drop my majorette baton, the woman who forbid me from square dancing & sock hops. The woman who said, "You better not let me find out you went to a dance, because if you do, you can move out!" Because dancing is a *sin*.

The next morning, I was good and ready to hear mom's apology—perhaps even admit her embarrassment—but I never heard a peep. She went about her day like nothing ever happened. Behavior like this made it very difficult for me to like her. I vented to my best friend Betty, telling her what I saw in full detail; She laughed at how gross it must have been to watch them bounce around like ponies.

The incident resulted in one positive though: Andy rented an apartment down the street for their future escapades, ensuring they'd never soil our mattresses again.

<u>Extra Duty</u>

The list of things required to keep mom satisfied never ended. In late high school, mom assigned me to help Lana, whose first-born child was colicky and had a rash on his balls. Lana was exhausted from dealing with the difficult child and Dave's work schedule didn't bring him home until well after midnight, so I'd show up after dinner and stay until Dave arrived—at which time he'd take me back home for a few hours sleep before school. The baby himself—Dave Jr—had a terrible rash that left his balls bright red and caused constant crying. The culprit was baby formula that he was somehow allergic to, so every time he peed it caused awful irritation of his balls that left them burning red like a fire hydrant. A solution was found by switching from formula to *goat's milk*, but it still took a few weeks for the rash to go away and relieve me of duty.

I managed to buy a used car in my senior year of high school through the kindness of a girlfriend's dad, who sold me his old jalopy for cheap. Gilbert used my car for his own extra duty: picking mom up after work. He'd wake up at 4am and drive to the post office, parking in the loading-dock alley to wait for mom's shift to end. More often than not, mom would come out to tell Gilbert she didn't need a ride—she was heading to breakfast with coworkers—resulting in Gilbert heading back home alone for a short nap before school. School meant nothing to mom— our personal time meant even less. In mom's mind, our only purpose was to serve her, and when we weren't serving her, we were serving Jesus.

Gilbert and I occasionally had extra duty together, like the day mom brought us with her to clean one of Andy's rentals: an upstairs apartment. When we arrived, I realized that Andy's wife and kids lived downstairs from the rental, and I was greatly annoyed since I knew they'd recognize us if they saw us—Andy's son had once confronted Gilbert at Colonial Tabernacle, telling Gilbert he hated him because *my dad loves you more than me.* Whatever mom's level of concern might have been —and it might have been zero—we went through with it, mopping, scrubbing, and sweeping Andy's vacancy as I stewed about how unfair it was. The incident said much about Andy and how he got his kicks.

Graduation

My graduation from Poly High School came in 1963, but like every other important date in my life, nobody celebrated. Mom didn't come to the ceremony, using the old reliable excuse that she couldn't take time off work. I wasn't surprised.

I hopped the city bus in my cap and gown, went down to the Municipal Auditorium on Ocean Boulevard, and graduated alone. No one was there to applaud when I walked across the stage to pick up my diploma, so I applauded myself. I felt rather ugly having nobody around to celebrate my graduation—the pimple breakout on my forehead didn't help matters.

Arriving home, there was no card from mom telling me how proud she was of my hard work, no recognition of me raising her boys while she played with her man. Her gift came the next morning—an early wakeup directing me to *"Get up and get a job, stop being a lazy bum."* I already had a part-time job, but mom told me I had to quit immediately and find a full-time position.

Colonial Tabernacle had a big dinner party for graduates every year—an event I'd looked forward to ever since I began attending church there. Unfortunately, the graduating class of 1963 was only one person—me—and I felt pretty jilted to be skipped over by the banquet. I hadn't quite been a model member of the congregation up to that point—there was my *I hate Jesus* moment, plus my friend Betty and I were the only rebellious girls prohibited from the choir since we wore makeup—but I still wanted to be treated like the kids who graduated before me. The steady string of missed birthdays and dances and graduations really bothered me. *Why must I always be the loser?*

One evening after graduation, Sister Taylor pulled me aside and handed me a box wrapped in a pretty pink bow. I opened it to find a beautiful purse from Knott's Berry Farm—it was my graduation gift. Sister Taylor knew the banquet forgot about me, but she remembered. Like all gifts, it was the thought that counted.

BELMONT AND THE LONG UNRAVEL

Shortly after my graduation, mom bought a two-bedroom house at 2201 Belmont Avenue. Gilbert and Mark once again shared a room, while mom and I shared the other—including the bed. Working hard enough to buy a house was surely a proud moment for mom, but for us it was just another pressure cooker.

Moving from Walnut to Belmont took us miles away from Andy's apartment—the love nest he rented after I caught him and mom having sex. With that distance came a more distant Andy, one who didn't show up to our home for weeks at a time. Mom entered a tailspin, spending her off days staring out the window and pacing the floor, waiting for Andy to stop by and spend an hour or two with her. "Where's Andy?" she'd ask, soon answering her own question with his predicted excuse, "He'll say he had a union meeting with employees, that's what he always says." I knew the writing was on the wall with Andy but I kept my beak shut—with mom you had to be careful not to challenge her too strongly, otherwise she'd turn everything upside down and make you the enemy.

Mom's suicide plans grew: In addition to running out the front door into oncoming traffic, she now intended to jump in the ocean and drown, ending her misery once and for all. When we asked, "What will we do if you die?" she'd reply, "It doesn't matter! You kids don't help me and don't keep the house clean." It was wacky and made no sense, but it kept us glued to her. Mom's life revolved around Andy, our lives revolved around her.

* * *

The rectangular object in Dr Lake's hand is flat, brown, and paper. It's a grocery bag, the kind checkout boys load your groceries in. Dr Lake snaps it open with a quick *wa-Pop!*

"Whenever she has an episode, place this paper bag over her head to calm her breathing," he instructs me and the boys in the examination room. Dr Lake illustrates by holding the opened bag above his head and gesturing downwards. He never actually wears the bag—that would be foolish.

Those were the doctor's orders for treating our hyperventilating mom. We referred to it as *bagging mom,* and it's exactly what we did when she became hysterical over Andy. Over the course of many years, an over-the-counter brown paper bag—non-prescription—was one of the tools we used to enable mom's hysteria. True to form, she never put the bag over her own head, because where's the fun in that? Mom's hysteria was much like Pentecostal hysteria—it only happened for an audience. And just like speaking in tongues never happens at a gas station on Tuesday morning, mom never hyperventilated in a fit of tears anywhere but at home—for us.

Coincidentally, mom also spoke in tongues for us—from the bathroom, sobbing. She kneeled for her prayers just like dad, moaning out peoples' name and begging Jesus to make their lives right by *her* standards. Did those people ask for prayer? Did she get their permission? Pentecostal arrogance showed itself again: Don't look at my sin—let's talk about *yours.*

Mom and her hostages

Mother's Little Helper

Mom's drama was extremely anxiety-inducing for us. It was our job to solve her problems, but she wouldn't allow a solution, so round and round we went in a loop of insanity. When mom's *Where's Andy?* windup eventually devolved into uncontrollable shaking and panting, Mark—who was still less than 12 years old —followed the doctor's other recommendation: "You just need your hormone shot mom," he reassured her. "You'll feel better after you get your shot." Then he bagged her.

Besides hormone shots and brown paper bags, Dr Lake had another tool in his bag for mom: *Valium.* She'd been medicated ever since dad died, and now her *Librium* was replaced with the newest drug in town. Mom's pills contributed greatly to her off-the-wall behavior, and were a likely contributor to the bane of our existence: Mom's lifelong diarrhea episodes.

Described by mom as *the scoots,* the first diarrhea attack occurred on the stool at work. Maybe she took an extra pill, maybe she skipped one—maybe it was just a bad cracker she had for lunch—but we were unpleasantly informed of yet another issue we had to fix for mom. We suggested that she take a roll of paper towels to work and line her underwear with them, anything to keep her safe and dry. The humor of it was lost on us though—the three kids who anxiously bit their nails hoping *mommy* wouldn't have more diarrhea at work.

Mom loopy on Valium

Like magic, the paper bags and diarrhea vanished once Andy reappeared. That was the true fix for mom's issues, but it was going away soon and she knew it.

Andy got divorced at some point in all of this—and this had been going for nearly ten years now—turning their affair into a mere casual relationship. Affairs have no competition, since the man's cheating is kept secret from his wife. Casual relationships, on the other hand, could have any number of other women—including new ones. To mom, any time not spent with her was time spent in the arms of another woman, and he was spending much less time with her nowadays. Still, she perked right up whenever he dropped in, and we were thankful for the reprieve from our misery.

* * *

Mom's erratic behavior was driving me nuts and I needed to get away from her. I now worked full-time at *North American,* and was actively dating. Predictably, mom disapproved of every guy I brought around—the same routine she had with Lana. It felt like mom wanted to keep me all to herself, which made sense considering my entire teenage life was spent raising the boys for her and listening to her god-awful whining about Andy. At the time, Gilbert also showed signs of leaving home, so if we both left, mom would be left alone with Mark—a child she'd have to raise herself.

My friend Betty set me up on a blind date with a man named Gary Deal, whose parents owned a real estate brokerage in Long Beach. I didn't particularly like him, but he proposed to me after five weeks and I accepted—too quick for mom to cancel him. Our wedding was set for a few weeks later.

The night before my wedding, I was washing dishes for mom at the kitchen sink and she asked me why the floors weren't clean. When I told her I didn't have time since I'd been touching up my wedding dress, she spanked me twice. It was not a joke.

The War is Lost

Living with mom was so bad that Gilbert volunteered for Vietnam to get away from her—or at least that's the joke I make. By 1967, me and Gilbert were both gone and mom had to change her work schedule from nights to days in order to care for Mark.

Andy still popped up every now and then; It seemed like he felt bad for mom and didn't know how to cut her loose. Maybe he had grander plans when their affair first began, but in the end their relationship boiled down to nothing but sex and a few daylight hours spent with the kids. Whatever Andy led her to believe, that's all it ever was for the ten years it lasted.

During the long unravel, I spotted Andy in the grocery store pushing a cart with another woman. It didn't surprise me—I'd figured him out long ago—but I never told mom because I knew it wouldn't matter.

I was once driving mom around on a Saturday morning when she spotted Andy's car with a redhead inside. "Hurry up and catch them!" she shouted, wanting to see the woman who stole her boyfriend. We never caught up to them, and wound up at the mall for pie & coffee as I listened to mom wonder what she did wrong with Andy. Mom felt she was much prettier than the redhead and couldn't understand what that woman had that she lacked. I told mom to forget about an answer because there wasn't any.

Andy ultimately married that redhead—also a woman with children of her own.

* * *

The year Andy divorced his original wife is unknown. Mom told the boys early on that he was divorced, but she never told me that and I was the one she confided in. It's a fair guess that his divorce occurred in 1962, the year Lana and Dave Copp were finally sponsored by Bethany Chapel to live in Japan as missionaries. We gave them a teary-eyed sendoff at San Pedro Harbor together with the Bethany Chapel wackos who hooted and hollered like monkeys as the big ocean liner sailed away. Mom even flew to Japan to stay with them for a month. Considering what came before, I doubt any of that could have happened if Andy was still a married man.

As for Andy, I think mom was too Christian for his taste. He liked trashy—Herb Alpert's whipped-cream girl springs to mind—and mom just wasn't trashy enough. She could give him all the money and love he wanted, but she still maintained a Christian identity that Andy knew all too well from being the brother of Colonial's pastor. However flawed mom's Christianity was, she still believed it, and that was the curse that doomed her and Andy.

Andy Taylor was a woman collector. He collected his wife and our mom, and collected other woman he wanted. Some of his behavior—like having us clean the apartment above his wife and children—was downright terrible, other moves (like talking up money problems to get a handout from mom) were questionable. I believe he had a harem stashed around the city—a handful of lonely ladies all waiting for their two hours a day with him. Andy could have broken it off with mom any time over the course of their ten-year relationship—he held all the cards and if he never showed again, it would have been over. But he kept appearing—he even showed up to my wedding. With a shift of perspective, Andy could easily be considered a creep.

Andy left mom with a parting gift: an adult dog named Yenta. Mom never liked animals and didn't care much for Yenta, but she accepted the dog. Even though Andy was gone for good, Yenta was her daily reminder of him, and any future suitors would be forced to wonder where the dog came from. Though it appeared throughout their relationship that mom clinged to Andy, in reality those roles were reversed—Andy's the one who couldn't let go.

Part III

Bob

MEET THE DEVIL

Mark was now the only child remaining under mom's roof, and it was a predictably terrible time for him. Since he was in junior high, mom was forced to change her work schedule from nights to days to supervise him. That meant more face time with mom—never a good thing.

Mom continued her practice of obnoxious bathroom prayers for Mark to hear. She called out sinners by name—identifying their sins in disgusting detail—then upped the ante with tongue speak. The bombardment of cries and moans kept Mark sheltering in his room from what was tantamount to psychological warfare.

Mark eventually found escape in high school sports, but athletics incurred injuries to which mom was entirely unsympathetic. After a football concussion sent him home, Mark relayed the coach's advice that he should visit a hospital. Mom told him he'd be fine—just take a nap. After badly spraining his knee in a baseball game, the coach wrapped it tightly and instructed him to lay up over the weekend. When Saturday morning arrived, mom rattled him out of bed and demanded he get outside to push-mow the lawn.

Mom's outrageous threats also continued. When cousins delivered sixteen-year-old Mark home an hour late on Friday night, mom pounced the moment he walked in the door, informing him that she'd had enough of his misbehavior and was calling the authorities on Monday to send him to foster care. Mark fell to his knees in tears, begging her for another chance. "Nope," she said, "I've had enough of you." Deathly afraid of being sent away—and without us as a buffer against mom—Mark continued pleading from his knees, but mom wouldn't have it. "I can't handle you anymore! I'm calling on Monday and they're taking you away!"

Mom's New Man

It was all smiles at work though. Mom's shift change came with a promotion to the Post Office's Stamps & Passport window. It was there that a romance blossomed with her new *romeo,* a mailman named Bob Ireland.

Originally from Cleveland, Ohio, Bob Ireland served on a destroyer in World War Two and *re-enlisted* for the Korean War. Or at least that's what he claimed. You see, Bob was a man whose stories never quite added up. To be fair, he did serve in the Korean War—but that's beside the point. Bob was universally disliked by everyone at the Post Office because Bob was a dishonest man. He couldn't lie about flesh and blood—three older children with ex-wife Vonda—but he lied about everything else.

By this time in early 1970, Gilbert had arrived back home from Vietnam and taken his own job at the Post Office. Coworkers warned Gilbert that Bob was sniffing around his mom, explaining that Bob was a loser and conman that Elsie should avoid at all costs. In contrast to Bob, mom was universally liked by coworkers who witnessed the Andy saga, and nobody wanted to see her taken advantage of again. They even warned her directly that Bob was big trouble, but their warnings fell on deaf ears—Elsie was in love again.

A few weeks into mom's new relationship, she called me and Gilbert to the Belmont house for a meet-and-greet with her new man. She was in great spirits and even had a pink blush to her cheeks. I had no forewarning of Bob and his reputation, so I was thrilled to meet this mystery man who'd come to rescue mom (and us) from all of her problems. Since mom's last guy was Andy—a handsome six-foot-one trombone player—I figured this one would be a step up. When the new guy arrived, he was a step down. A huge step down.

Bob Ireland was a short man—so short that his feet dangled from tall chairs. His head carried a big coif of dark greasy hair; below that hair stared a pair of dark eyes topped by bushy eyebrows. His nose was thick, and he sported a permanent smirk begging to be smacked any time of day. Worse than the smirk was his smile —it was missing a front tooth.

Bob looked me in the eye and saw that I wasn't impressed. His vibe made my skin crawl and I couldn't believe mom was serious about him. The man looked like the Devil—before long, he'd prove he was.

As she'd done since I was a teenager, mom asked me for relationship advice. She never really wanted advice—mom couldn't care less what any of us thought—she only wanted to pick out the things she agreed with. Unfortunately with Bob, I couldn't conjure anything nice to say. He wasn't handsome, he wasn't charming— the man didn't even have all his teeth. Knowing mom's preference in men, I was floored that she settled for the complete opposite with Bob.

What I didn't know yet was that Bob had the same thing Andy had that worked so well on mom—the gift of lying. After dad, mom liked men who lied because it connected with the wild side she couldn't allow herself to live. Though mom projected naivete with men, in reality she was very smart and quickly figured out what Andy was up to the whole time; When Bob's turn came, she figured that out, too. But in mom's upside-down world, she wanted these scheming men to lie to her—it was the truth she didn't want to hear. With Bob, she'd soon get all the lies she could stand.

Burning with Lust

Fast approaching fifty-years old, mom was swept off her feet by Bob. Within a few weeks of our meet-and-greet, she disclosed to Mark that they were both *burning with lust.* Mark knew what that meant, but just in case he *didn't,* she reminded him one steamy night in front of Belmont as the two lovebirds went at it in a parked car. Mark would have been happily oblivious to the event had it not been for the periodic honking of the car's horn on their quiet neighborhood street. He looked out the window to investigate the honking and his eyes immediately settled on the disgusting and forever-frozen image of mom and Bob having sex. *Honk!*

The next morning, mom confronted Mark about *her own* misdeeds, pointing a finger at him and stating that they "wanted to have fun like everyone else." She went further, announcing that they were getting married and would soon live together. Surprised, Mark posed a few basic questions about his soon-to-be stepfather. In true mom fashion, her response was to walk out of the room.

The Devil Finds Jesus

In love again and with marriage in the wind, mom went back to church. Colonial Tabernacle must have found it exceedingly strange that their newest member was the former mistress of the pastor's brother, but soap operas were all the rage in 1970, and now the church got their very own courtesy of the Rasmussens.

Mom's only requirement for marriage was that Bob convert to Christianity. In the Pentecostal world, there are no mandatory rites for becoming a Christian. If you have a cold water fetish, you can request a baptism and have your head dunked— or you can skip it. If you like being the center of attention, you can request a stage performance where a collection of plump hands will touch your head while you cry your guts out for the whole world to see—or you can skip it. Bob skipped it.

The Christian conversion of Bob Ireland consisted of simply attending church with mom and showing his face to the congregation. It was easy money—made even easier after mom paid to install a new tooth in his head. Bob lifted his short arms to the sky and praised Jesus so mom could see how good he was doing—I watched him smirk throughout and saw how full of shit he was.

Mom's coworkers begged her to stay away from this man

Coworkers and family desperately tried talking mom out of marrying Bob, but the Devil had her snared and there was no shaking him off. A wedding date was set for October 31st, 1970—Halloween Night.

Wedding Night Blues

As mom's trusted confidante, I was the wedding coordinator and followed her wish for a full-service affair with candles, flowers, and an organist. The color theme was *Seventies Pink* to match the cheeks of the blushing bride.

Officiating the wedding was Pastor Orvel Taylor, Andy's brother. Bob knew exactly who Orvel was, and how embarrassing this whole thing looked to everyone in attendance. The joke was on Elsie.

As I perfected my maid-of-honor dress in the upstairs dressing room, mom suddenly entered in a panic. I asked what was wrong and she mumbled, "I don't know what to do?"

After the unnecessary but required back-and-forth with mom, she explained that Bob confessed to a prior marriage whose divorce might not be final, which would make their imminent marriage invalid. Maybe. Or maybe not. Bordering on hysteria, mom asked me point-blank if she should go ahead with the wedding.

Her question was yet another in a long line of *please lie to me* moments; I'd learned mom's methods long ago, and knew she'd go through with it regardless of my answer. The real question for me was, "Do we do this the easy way, or the hard way?" I chose the easy way—Yes, you should go ahead with the wedding.

Freed from the hard decisions, mom walked down the aisle in sweet wedding bliss —not a trace of concern on her face. Halloween-night vows were exchanged, the couple kissed, and Bob & Elsie Ireland became God's newest couple. The reception's refreshments were a weird Halloween blend of nuts, cake, and mints.

Bob's grand honeymoon plan was an overnight stay in the Big Bear Mountains —a short three-hour drive from Long Beach—but the romantic evening mom envisioned with her new husband was thwarted since Bob brought an extra bag with him—a bag named Anna Ireland.

Strangers were never surprised to learn that Anna was Bob's mom, because Anna looked just like him. Same eyes, same eyebrows, same nose—even her smirk was the same. On that honeymoon drive up to the beautiful mountains of Big Bear, Anna rode up front since she got car sick driving around curves. Bob's new bride, Elsie Ireland, sat in the back seat—with the groceries.

On arrival to their Big Bear cottage, Bob and his mother unpacked their bag of groceries, pulling out a big clump of bananas, donuts, and instant coffee. The donuts and coffee were for everyone's morning breakfast, but the fruit was for Anna—mommy loved bananas.

With nothing to do on her honeymoon night, mom sat and watched Anna fill up on bananas as Bob climbed into bed after a long day. When Anna finished up and retired to her separate bedroom, mom had her first chance with Bob—the man she'd married only three hours ago. He was out like a light. Nothing could rouse him—not mom's gentle coos, nor the grinding snores from Anna's nose that tore through the thin wall like a chainsaw all night. The only participant in the Ireland honeymoon was mom, who spent the evening talking to God.

* * *

Mom's house on Belmont was sold after a week of marriage; She told nobody about the pending sale. The buyer was my old high school friend Betty and her husband, who also said nothing about it. The brokers selling the house were my in-laws, the Deal family—they also said nothing. The sale of mom's house was a big secret, and for good reason: Mom gave the proceeds to Bob, who supposedly needed it to save his Molino Avenue property from foreclosure.

Bob's property at 290 Molino Ave was a fourplex, with three upstairs units in the rear and a large downstairs unit up front that was occupied by Bob, his mother, and college-age son Bob Jr. The rear units had tenants, some of whom were single women—whether those renters paid Bob with *money* was anyone's guess.

No evidence exists that Bob was actually losing Molino to the bank—all we had was mom's word, and when it came to Bob, who knows what the truth was. Bob could have lied to her, she could have lied to us, or maybe the bank was really going to foreclose. The only certainty was that the secret sale of Belmont marked the start of a *bang your head against the wall* roller-coaster that mom forced us to ride with her—we never knew we could say no.

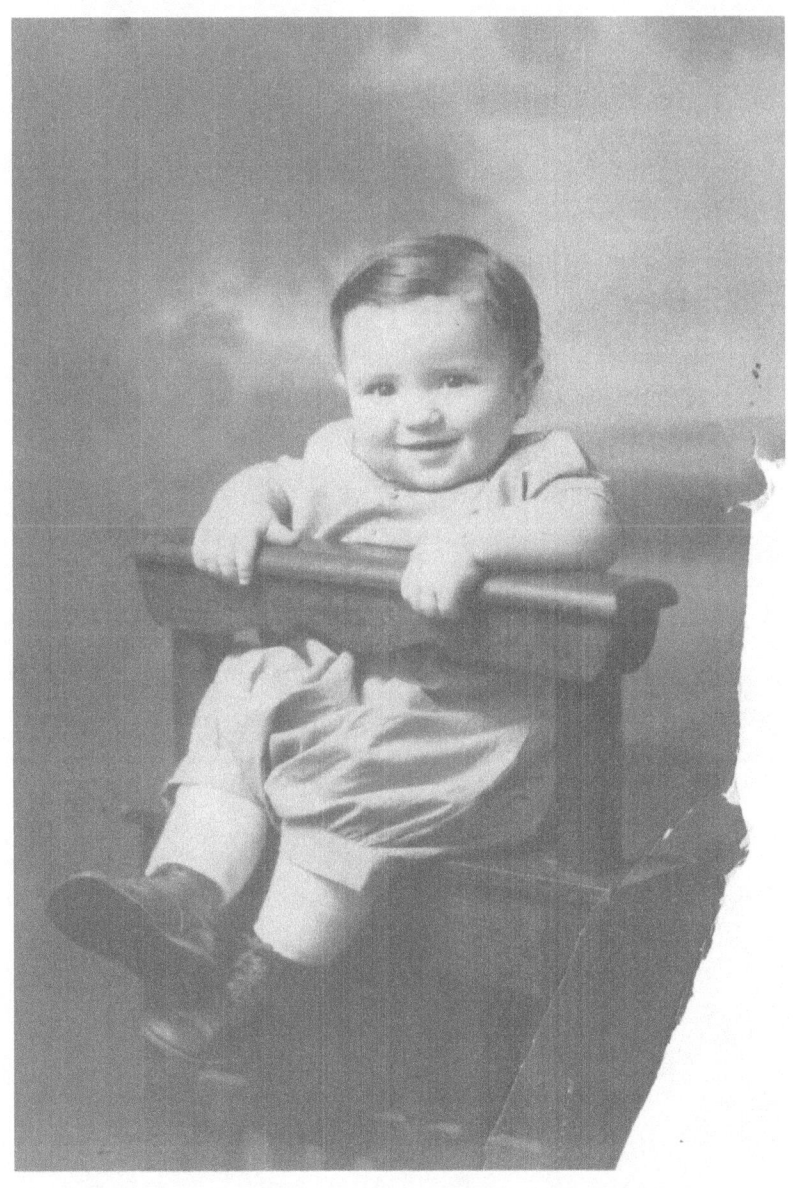

I wouldn't even trust Bob as a baby

The Halloween Wedding

Bob's banana-lovin' mom Anna honeymooned with her son

ROBBIE THE RODENT

Mom and Mark moved in with Bob and his family at Molino. The setup was awkward at first: it's not every day that two 18 & 20 year old men are forced to become stepbrothers *and* cohabitate, but it worked because Bob Jr was everything his dad was not. Extremely kind, extremely smart, and capable as any man could be, Junior soon became a friend to Mark. More importantly, he offered words of caution about his father.

Junior told Mark that the unknown woman his dad married—the one that nearly upended mom's wedding—was a drug-addicted prostitute. His dad tried divorcing her but for whatever reason (and there were many), Junior wasn't sure if the divorce was finalized.

He offered a further warning to Mark: Don't let my dad touch your mom's money. Junior even told mom directly not to let his dad into her bank and credit accounts. The young college man had seen it all before with his own mother Vonda, and didn't want Elsie—whom he adored—falling prey to his father. Unfortunately, as well as Junior knew his dad, he obviously knew nothing about our mom.

Diarrhea Saturdays

With me and Gilbert out of the house, mom shifted gears on how she controlled us. Saturdays were the designated day when one of us—usually me—tended to mom. It wasn't optional and there was no missing it—not even for pregnancy. If I gave birth on a Tuesday (births that mom never attended), I'd still be there on Saturday to pick her up. If I was heading to Palm Springs for vacation, you can bet I made sure someone was around to cover for me. Her tool to ensure someone arrived on Saturday was one we knew all too well—diarrhea.

Perhaps the most urgent of words, diarrhea was mom's bat signal letting us know that she needed help pronto—full lights and sirens. No person on the planet discussed their own diarrhea more than mom, and we reacted accordingly, showing up at her door with Kaopectate even though she was fully capable of treating herself. Mom didn't treat her own diarrhea for the same reason she didn't bag her own hyperventilating head when we lived with her: *control*. Diarrhea was the wildcard mom used to keep us forever on edge and bound to her.

Every Saturday didn't bring diarrhea though, sometimes she was perfectly regular —like the afternoon when mom proudly announced to me that she'd put Bob in charge of her money. Exactly what Junior warned her not to do.

Where's Bob?

The Irelands had only been married a couple months when one of them disappeared—it was Bob, and mom was distraught.

Mark, Gilbert and I gathered in Molino's kitchen as mom sat on a stool and tearfully explained that she'd paid for Bob to go on a retreat to *Israel* with televangelist Rex Humbard. The first leg of the trip was in Florida, where Bob flew to meet up with fellow travelers. He'd been gone now for two weeks—a week overdue—and hadn't called.

It was a bizarre story that made no sense. Aside from play-acting in church, Bob wasn't religious; his knowledge of Rex Humbard must have come from the *Christian Broadcasting Network* that mom was a frequent viewer of. But going to Israel? Bob?

Junior was livid. He called Rex Humbard's ministry in Florida to track down his dad but was told they'd never heard of him. It was the same routine Junior had gone through with his own mom. We left that evening without an answer, feeling terrible for our mom whose new husband had already skipped out on her.

And then one day, all was fine. Bob called Junior requesting pickup from the airport, and mom received him at home with a hero's welcome. She never told us where Bob was because she never would have asked. Maybe Bob really went to Israel. Maybe he only went to Florida. Maybe he went to Vegas. Nobody knew but Bob.

Blues for Mark

In 1972, after a year or so under the Ireland's roof, Mark busied himself with school at Long Beach City College and a part-time job at Taco Bell. His older peer, Junior, was on a different trajectory, wrapping up a university degree with an eye to medical school. Mark came home every night to hear Junior playing music with his mouth—a saxophone. In a normal home, Junior may have bleated out *Green*

Junior (seated next to Dave Copp) played sax and warned us about his dad

Onions or *Yakety Sax,* but the Ireland home was off kilter, filled with unbalanced adults who lied and cheated and ate bananas like no tomorrow. For them, Junior played the blues.

The Prized Son & The Other One

Shortly thereafter, Junior was heading to South Carolina for medical school and needed a car for cross-country travel. Mom—who had a habit of preferring everyone else's children over her own—was all too ready to offer hers. She and Bob could make due with Bob's truck. Elsie's selflessness was one of many reasons Junior adored his stepmother, and he can't be faulted for accepting the offer.

After Junior moved to South Carolina, fate saw to it that Mark's used car broke down. With full-time city college, part-time employment, athletics, and church, Mark was a hustler who couldn't rely on public transport to make things work.

He applied for a college loan, planning to use those funds for school while his paycheck paid for a replacement car. Since Mark still lived with his *parents,* they needed to co-sign for the loan.

Bob refused to sign for Mark. Excuses were offered but none were legitimate. When Mark turned to mom—hoping to find the same selflessness afforded to Junior—she bee-lined out of the room. Mark wouldn't be getting a loan.

* * *

The strange Ireland marriage continued its volatility into the mid-70s. Bob would disappear for a weekend, mom would sound the shit alarm, then when he finally showed up she'd wave us off. We were powerless to confront him because mom forbid us from intervening, casually laughing off our threats and changing the subject once she got the desired attention. Mom consistently ramped us up and down over Bob, just like she did with Andy. I dreaded hearing the phone ring, because I knew it was mom calling to suck me in to another Bob problem—and I knew that whatever the problem was, Bob was somewhere smirking about it. I so desperately wanted to smack the smirk off his face.

Imagine my elation when Bob's ex-wife Vonda did indeed smack him—and in public. According to mom, she and Bob were at a fast-food restaurant eating dinner when Vonda walked inside, went straight to their table, and launched one across his face. Vonda pointed at mom with a warning, "You'll be sorry for trusting him!" then stormed out. Crafty old Bob immediately spun it as hilarious, telling mom that Vonda was jealous she couldn't have him anymore. Mom related the story to me with laughter; she really believed Vonda wanted him back.

Bob's Heart Attacks Him

Up until 1975, Bob was a full-time mailman whose regular disappearances were made to fit around his work schedule. Occasional vacations with mom did occur however, including a trip to Japan to visit Lana & Dave Copp and their young family. As one would expect, the Copps didn't like Bob, but that didn't matter— Bob was used to people disliking him. Even his own heart didn't like him, as was proved when he had a mild heart attack at home. He survived, but it was enough to get him retired early from the Post Office. Bob must have loved it—now he could disappear at will.

* * *

In the latter half of the 70s, a reshuffling took place for the Rasmussens. All of us were now married with children. I dropped my first Gary and married a second one. Mark had become yet *another* Rasmussen mailman, and Gilbert—Roy's eldest son—assumed dad's mantle, quitting his job and moving to Visalia (in the Central Valley) to retrace dad's steps in ministry. Mom was extremely supportive of Gilbert's move, visiting him regularly to provide financial support towards his ministerial ambitions.

The Copp family also flew home from Japan in the late-70s, roosting back at Bethany Chapel where Dave Copp was next-in-line to the throne. Lana began joining us for Saturday lunch at mom's favorite restaurant—a coffee-stenched place inside the Lakewood Mall called *Clifton's Cafeteria*. Clifton's was sort of like a buffet for poor people: You grabbed a tray and shuffled down the line to assemble your *a la carte* meal. Want ham, corn, and green jello? It's yours, $3.85. Turkey, spinach, and mashed potatoes? Be our guest, $4.55. Three sides of macaroni? You got it pal, $0.90. As Saturday afternoon regulars, we knew Clifton's well and were very comfortable there, perhaps a little too comfortable—my wedding reception for the Second Gary was held there.

Bob's mom Anna was also shuffled out in the late 70s, returning home to Cleveland where the bananas were less fresh. Replacing her on Molino's couch was mom's sister Thelma, a lovely woman who was terminally ill with emphysema. Thelma didn't let emphysema stop her from smoking, and I loved her for it. She was a warm, kind Lutheran who showed no trace of the Pentecostal arrogance I'd known so well growing up.

Unfortunately, Thelma's kindness was exploited by Bob, who constantly hit her up for money while driving her to doctor's appointments throughout the week. Thelma politely complained to mom (and me) that Bob kept asking her for money; Mom replied that she was confused and it was the other way around—terminally-ill Thelma was actually asking *Bob* for money.

Mom and Bob Show Off

One warm Saturday morning, I arrived at Molino to pick mom up for our regular *Clifton's* lunch with Lana. After receiving no response to my door knock, I knocked again. Still getting no response, I opened the door and went inside. Mom usually waited for me in the kitchen, but this time she wasn't there. I ventured towards the rear bedroom and saw Bob lying on the bed smirking. I followed his eyeline to see mom in the adjoining bathroom, naked on all fours and scrubbing the tub with a toilet brush. Once again, mom was naked in front of me with her butt hanging

Mom's sister Thelma complained that Bob kept asking her for money.

down around her knees. I asked her to put some clothes on and retreated to the living room to wait.

This was a replay of when I caught her and Andy having sex in the boy's bedroom, but with one key difference: Mom didn't hurry out of the room whispering *sorry* this time. In fact, she and Bob laughed at my reaction—Bob especially. They both knew I was coming over and decided to give me a surprise. Mom was all smiles as we left for Clifton's, never saying a word about what happened. She got me *again*.

Robbie the Rodent

From the moment I met him, Bob gave me bad vibes. He knew I didn't like him and knew I couldn't do a damn thing about it since mom was wrapped up in his spell. This was a man who told mom on their wedding night that he wasn't divorced, took her on an overnight honeymoon with his *mother*, then shortly thereafter disappeared for two weeks to a secret location. If mom would put up with that, she'd put up with anything—and he knew it. Even if mom wanted to leave, where would she go? She already sold her house and Bob was on her bank accounts and credit cards. The most we could do was come up with an insulting nickname for him, coined by Mark and Gilbert: *Robbie the Rodent*. The man was vermin.

* * *

With mom in the bag, Bob's eyes wandered to the ladies surrounding her: Mark & Gilbert's wives Debbie & Dawn, and me—who he fixated on. Bob told my hairdresser Gene at *Mane Designs* that he dreamed of me and Debbie as an ice-cream sandwich with him in the middle. Bob invited us girls to dinner, where he brought jewelry from his supposed international travels, once gifting me what he claimed were emeralds from *Colombia.* I took them to a pawn shop for assessment. "These are indeed emeralds," the owner told me, "Cheap ones." Did Bob really bring emeralds back from Colombia, or did he buy them on a trip to the Mexican border with mom? Maybe he bought them at the Sears jewelry counter—who knows?

After a claimed trip to England, Bob had *English China* delivered to mom with instructions to forward to me as a gift. Mom was very annoyed to give me that big cardboard box full of china, because she was the one footing the bill for it. I pawned it just like I pawned the emeralds, and once again learned that Bob's gift was junk. Did he really buy *English China* in England and have it shipped, or did he just order it through a mail-order catalog? Did he ever go to England in the first place?

At the time, we all firmly believed that Bob traveled to these international destinations, even concocting our own pet story that he was a *jewel smuggler.* In hindsight however, there's no evidence that Bob visited these places. Not a picture, not a postcard, no jet lag, nothing but his own lying tongue and the word of mom who constantly covered for him.

Suspect #1

Somewhere along the way, mom & Bob bought a rental home at 2103 East 6th Street—the same Bethany Chapel neighborhood we lived in so long ago. After I married the Second Gary, we rented this home and stayed for a couple years. It was there that we experienced an odd chain of events that makes Bob an even more suspicious character in hindsight:

Event 1:

Saturday morning, 7am. Lying in bed next to the Second Gary, I'm awoken by a sound in our hallway. I get up to investigate the noise and see Bob in our bathroom.

"Bob, what are you doing here?" I ask.

"Oh sorry, I thought you'd already be gone for the day."

"At seven in the morning?"

Bob had used his landlord key to enter the house, and claimed to be doing maintenance to our bathroom, something we hadn't requested —certainly not at 7am on a Saturday morning while we were asleep. What was Bob up to?

Event 2:

On a Saturday afternoon a couple weeks after the bathroom incident, my dog Norman alerted me to smoke coming from the house. I ran outside to see fire around my bedroom window. The fire department arrived to extinguish the flames, and after a quick investigation they showed me where someone had wedged paper and cloth into the window frame and lit it with a match. They called it arson.

A decade earlier, a church in Long Beach attended by Bob's ex-wife Vonda was intentionally burned down. Arson investigators asked the pastor if he suspected anyone—Bob Ireland was named. The police questioned Bob, and although another man was eventually arrested for the crime, Junior felt suspicious enough about his own father to disclose this to Mark. Junior also said his dad crafted meticulous fires in the Molino fireplace and enjoyed watching them burn.

Event 3:

In a span of six months, two of my cars were stolen, one of which was later found at a chopshop in LA. Considering that Bob was once married to a drug-addicted prostitute, might he have networked with people who steal cars for a living?

Event 4:

My dog Norman—the good boy who alerted me to the bedroom fire— went missing on a weekday. Since Norman was a large Labrador, I had to leave him in the backyard during the day. Since our backyard fence was dilapidated, I'd secure him to a tree with a long chain so he couldn't get out—something I feel terrible about now as a dog grandma, but at the time I thought it was better than leaving him inside the stuffy house all day. Regardless, when I came home from work, Norman was gone.

A couple days later I got a phone call: Norman had been found in the *San Bernardino Mountains*—the same mountains where Bob took mom for their honeymoon. A good samaritan found Norman tied to a tree and called me through the number on his tag. Norman was soon back home with us—but not for long.

Event 5:

My kids came home from school one day and found Norman dead—strangled by the long chain attached to the tree. I'd had Norman since he was a puppy—he'd never had an issue with his chain before.

In the moment, I couldn't see all of these things happening to me—it was just another bad year of mom's diarrhea, made worse by stolen cars and missing dogs and burning windows and Bob's smirk. In retrospect, the simplest answer to all of it was Bob.

Bob wasn't in my house at 7am to fix a toilet, he was creeping around and peeping in my bedroom. The Saturday afternoon fire at my bedroom window wasn't set by a stranger in broad daylight, it was set by suspected arsonist Bob Ireland to harass me and my husband. One car stolen, okay—but two cars in six months? And my good boy Norman didn't *hitch-hike* up to the mountains, and he certainly didn't wander there and tie himself to a tree—Bob just let himself into my backyard to take friendly Norman for a ride. When Norman returned, so did Bob. My grown puppydog didn't strangle himself, it was Bob—the *Devil*.

Robbie the Rodent

TRAINWRECK

Mom's whining about Bob got progressively worse as their marriage entered the 80s, especially the sexual nature of it that I was always so disappointed to hear about. One recurring complaint concerned mom's cervical cancer in 1972 that was treated by radiation implants (a procedure called brachytherapy). Mom sobbed that Bob had refused sex with her since then, using the excuse that he didn't want to *catch cancer.* How was I to respond? Another Saturday arrived, and now she was crying about the porno magazines she found in Bob's truck. His excuse was that someone must have *planted them there* to frame him. Bob went further with it, claiming his feelings were hurt that mom would accuse him of such a thing.

Separate from sex were the money issues. Bob constantly took trips on mom's dime, occasionally name-dropping the pastors he claimed to be helping by guiding their church group on an international tour. Mom wasn't invited on these international trips, of course, and as with all of his escapades, no pictures or postcards ever returned home with him. The only thing mom got was the bill.

They did go on a few vacations together—an Alaskan cruise, a border run to Mexico, a visit to mom's friends in South Dakota—but these were just bones Bob threw to the woman he referred to as the *Big E.* In reality, Bob had no interest in doing anything alone with the *Big E*—she was his moneybag and nothing more. The real action was elsewhere.

Spy Games

Bob was so strange and mysterious that a couple church friends spent a weekend tailing him around town to figure out what he did all day, an effort which proved futile as Bob engaged in the mundane chores of a retiree; What our naive friends didn't consider was that Bob's action would have occurred *at night.* Sailor Bob was far and away more world savvy than the average church goober whose entire life occurred within the restricted bubble of Christianity. It would take far better than a couple binocular-toting knuckleheads to trip Bob up.

Slowly but surely, Bob spent all of mom's money.

Downsizing

In 1980, mom & Bob sold the 6th Street house, so I moved my family into one of Molino's rentals. That lasted until 1981, when they sold that, too. Without Molino for themselves, mom & Bob moved to the Kotobuki apartments on 2nd Street.

Selling these two properties (including the one they lived in) reflected on mom & Bob's money issues. Separate from Bob's spending, mom also provided financial support to her and Gilbert's dream of a Visalia ministry, an endeavor that eventually failed and brought Gilbert back to Long Beach in 1982. Mom was wrapped up in the Visalia mission right from the start, regularly visiting Gilbert's rented hall to cheer on the recreation of what she and Roy did decades ago. As the eldest son of a preacher man, Gilbert didn't have much choice in the matter—the torch was his whether he wanted it or not. Arriving back in Long Beach, Gilbert and mom doubled-down with another new church, this one in Harbor City operated under the auspices of Colonial Tabernacle. Its name had a great ring to it—Harbor Tabernacle—but with a Rasmussen at the helm, it was doomed to fail.

Meanwhile, full-time mailman Mark was getting his own sobering education in church. He'd spent the past few years driving to LA for night classes at *Life Bible*

College; When Mark finally graduated, he learned that his degree was worthless. Mark enjoyed academics and had his sights set on a Master's Degree—now he'd have to start from scratch.

Around this time, mom & Bob also secretively bought a second-floor condo on Junipero Street. Mark wasn't aware of the condo but Gilbert knew about it, as did I since mom pointed it out to me when we drove past on Saturdays. She'd instruct me to drive slowly, then try in vain to peer through the second-floor windows: Mom thought Bob had a girl living there, but she couldn't check because Bob held the keys and forbid her from visiting.

The secret Junipero condo was likely purchased with the intention of mom & Bob both living there after selling Molino. Instead, they wound up at the Kotobuki apartments while Bob used the condo for whatever he was up to. Mom's life and finances were steadily shrinking as Bob drove them into the ground.

Police Arrive for Bob

Things got mighty hairy for Bob when the police came knocking one Sunday morning. Mom was startled by their presence, but Bob coolly assured her that he knew what they wanted and directed her to stay in the bedroom while he handled it. After they left, Bob filled her in on the situation:

> Bob had recently been in San Diego on business—checking out potential investment property—when he witnessed a girl get hit by a car while walking on the side of the road. The car fled the scene, but Bob remained to help the girl and provide a witness statement to police. The hit-and-run driver was later arrested and Bob was now being subpoenaed as a witness in the case. Bob Ireland was a hero.

When mom related this story to us the following Saturday at *Clifton's,* she was filled with pride that her Bob did the right thing and would soon perform his civic duty by supporting the girl in a San Diego courtroom. Mom was actually quite irritated that the police showed up the way they had, since it caused neighbors to gossip about them. When I pressed for more details on San Diego, she turned her annoyance on me: I was ruining a perfectly good lie—why won't I just accept it?

The real story came out later from Junior. The truth was that Bob picked up a hooker in San Diego and got caught in a sting operation. He had to go to court alright—to appear in front of a judge and plead guilty to solicitation. This wasn't a story fit for mom's ears, of course, so we didn't tell her. It wouldn't have mattered anyways, because whenever we tried pinning Bob down for his behavior, mom walked out of the room. Mom didn't care about the truth, she wanted the lies. As long as Bob kept the truth just out of reach from her—like what really existed inside the locked Junipero condo—she plastered a smile on her public face while her private face heaped misery upon us.

* * *

In 1984, Bob advised mom to retire from the Post Office at age 62 to enjoy the good life with him. She took his advice, then proceeded to have a nervous breakdown a few months later. Whatever romantic dream Bob sold her never materialized; Instead, mom found herself trapped at home alone, tormented by her own thoughts.

Mom's solution was to set a new precedent: staying with my family at 6142 East Keynote Street. She settled into our den, where she slept on the couch and moped around feeling sad for herself—Diarrhea Saturdays came to me.

She still stole all the attention for herself, especially on Saturdays when Gilbert visited with his family. Before lunch at *Clifton's,* we'd all gather around my kitchen table as mom moaned on and on about Bob disappearing again. She punctuated her (and our) misery by laying her head on the table, face down. On one of these occasions, Gilbert's wife Dawn finally reached her limit and stormed out to the front yard; A few minutes later she hollered in through our kitchen window, "*You people are cra-zy! Cra-zy!*" Dawn's assessment was proven correct once the clock hit 11:30am—that's when mom ceased all grief and announced it was time to see Lana at Clifton's. To mom's credit, she always paid.

The way mom turned from hot to cold is the same way she disappeared when Bob returned. She'd be on my couch for days at a time, then suddenly she was gone. No note, no phone call, no thank you—she just vanished and that was that. When I'd see her for Saturday lunch, she was all smiles, never saying a word about her disappearance. I once confronted her about it: Why do you suddenly leave and not tell me where you went? Mom pooh-poohed my question and weaseled out of an answer—there was no winning with her.

Mom eventually took a teller job at the *Long Beach Postal Credit Union,* a perfect fit since it brought her back into regular contact with Post Office friends. The extra income was also good considering how much it cost to support Bob and his bogus expeditions, including the one sponsored by Gilbert's fledgling church: Harbor Tabernacle.

Pastor Gilbert

The Harbor Tabernacle was Gilbert's second church venture and received the official blessing of Colonial Tabernacle. The majority-black congregation was only about thirty people, and whether it would succeed or not was a big question. Considering Bob Ireland's involvement with it, the chances were zero.

Mom and Gilbert reliving dad at Harbor Tabernacle

Mom was a major supporter of Gilbert's ventures, and Bob had a crafty way of always working himself into the church scene, so when the idea of an Africa trip lead by Bob was proposed, mom was all for it. As we understood it later, Bob led a contingent of talented young women to South Africa where they embarked on a *singing tour* of local churches. Since Harbor Tabernacle had virtually no money coming in, funding for the trip came from one person—mom.

The South Africa trip was, as usual, secretive. Mark and I rarely attended Gilbert's church since we had our own lives at Colonial, so our knowledge of the big Africa trip came from mom and Gilbert well after the fact. As was the case with all of Bob's international adventures, there was no evidence that he ever went to Africa, and this story in particular defies belief. Mom certainly *paid* for a trip, but where did the money go?

Despite the dubious African safari, mom had a grand ol' time at Harbor Tabernacle. She loved reliving her glory days by playing the organ and singing with Gilbert, whose soprano voice was similar to Roy. Bob got in on the action too, doing handyman work and engaging in his one true love: wallpapering. Bob had a serious fetish for papering walls and was damn good at it—perhaps it's how he covered up blood spatter.

Gilbert leaned on Mark to attend his church—even floating the idea of Mark selling his Long Beach house to buy a nearby condo—but Mark was content to keep his home and just drive to Harbor City on Sundays. Those trips proved short-lived: After a year, Colonial Tabernacle pulled support for their sister church by defrocking Gilbert. A great many reasons could be listed for his defrocking and even more theorized—Bob & Gilbert's *Great African Safari* couldn't have been popular among higher-ups—but the end result was that mom & Gilbert's dream of retracing Roy's footsteps was over for good. The Harbor Tabernacle had capsized.

* * *

The summer of 1986 was hot, made even hotter because mom was back on my couch with a broken ankle. The ankle wasn't her reason for staying though—it was Bob again.

Dave Copp was now in charge at Bethany Chapel, and mom attended his Wednesday night church service alone since the Copps didn't like Bob. Mom was dropped off and picked up by Bob, who must have been greatly annoyed that mom was cutting into his Wednesday night action with *church bullshit.*

According to mom, Bob picked her up after service and proceeded to run out of gas on the shortish journey from Bethany Chapel to the Kotobuki Apartments. They both exited the truck to walk home; Bob moved quickly along the sidewalk while mom struggled behind on crutches. Upset that she was taking so long, Bob began punching mom's arm to get her moving quicker.

That was mom's story for why she was back on my couch. Whether it was true or not, who knows? Mom showed me no bruises, and it's difficult to believe Bob forced her to crutch down a sidewalk at night because he ran out of gas on a drive so short he could have coasted it. Mom made a habit of covering for Bob, although this wasn't covering unless the true story was far worse—and maybe it was. The only thing I knew was true—beyond any doubt—was that I was tired of this crap, and it was getting worse.

Please Don't Leave Me

In the terminal part of their marriage, mom kicked it up a notch. Whether it was Bob disappearing on open-ended trips to Ohio, Bob disappearing to parts unknown, or Bob in the flesh and punching her arm, the end result was always mom in a heap on my couch. I'd get ready for work on Monday morning and see her teary eyes staring at me from a corner of the den:

"Please don't go," she cried.

"I have to go mom, it's my job."

"But you're like my mother. Please stay—don't leave me."

That's the conversation I'd have before leaving to drop my son off at school and start the workday. It was very difficult. *Very.* Then I'd come home and she'd be gone—poof. *Guess I'll see her Saturday.*

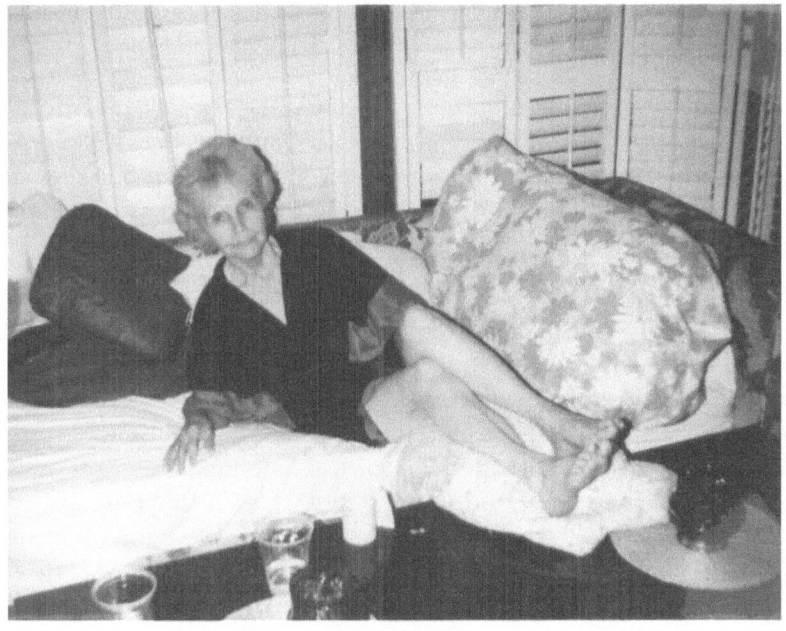

Mom on my couch after another Bob disappearance

Bob's Downfall

Bob finally messed up one day and did the unforgivable. Bob could lie about his women and lie about his travels, but in late-1986, Bob couldn't lie about his Hepatitis B.

Bob's illness was so serious that he was hospitalized for it. He tried to hide it, but the hospital notified his son Junior, who in turn notified us. Unlike Bob's secret condo and suspected trysts, this truth was no longer out of reach for mom. She decided to drop him—which meant putting her adult children on the highest alert status. It was battle stations for the Rasmussens.

Everyone showed up to move mom out of the Kotobuki Apartments: me, Gilbert, Mark, and our spouses. Mom was panicked that Bob would arrive home during the move, and asked me to call the hospital to check his status. He was still there—but being released later that day. Now we all were panicked, insistent that we had to get mom out quickly, or else. None of us asked the question, *"Or else what?"*

Mom was perfectly free to take her belongings and leave the apartment. Even if Bob showed up, what's he gonna do? He was always scared of men, and we had three of them with us. Our panic was merely a symptom of our upbringing, a conditioned response to mom's controlling behavior towards her three children—now adults in their late thirties.

We moved mom's stuff into my garage and took our seats for the kitchen-table moanfest, including Mark who was normally absent on Saturdays since he worked carrying mail. We were happy that mom finally got away from Bob though, even if their future was still uncertain. If mom wanted to be a thankless basket case with us this time, that was okay—it was worth it.

Bethany Chapel's New Boss

The cream had finally risen to the top and Dave Copp was now in charge of Bethany Chapel. With the mean old bastard David Schoch retired and Gilbert's Harbor Tabernacle resting at the bottom of the ocean, the Rasmussen family reconvened at Bethany Chapel with the Copps. Commingling our previously-distant families was a good time, made even better by Dave's easygoing style and wit. Some ideas didn't work of course, but that's what made Dave fun. Whether it be *dancing in the spirit* down the aisles on Sunday morning (aka the Christian Conga Line), or ringing in the New Year with a banner proclaiming *"Let's Go To Heaven in '87!"* it was the complete opposite of Prophet Schoch's finger-in-your-face style, and a refreshing take on what Christianity should be. It wouldn't last long.

* * *

A year passed without Bob and we were ecstatic that mom stayed away from him. I wasn't thrilled to have her on my couch, but that was a small price to pay for the greater pain avoided. Mom still kept in touch with him because she'd give me occasional updates: The secret Junipero condo was long gone, foreclosed on and taken after Bob stopped paying the mortgage. Now he lived at the *Long Beach Motor Lodge* on Long Beach Boulevard, a motel occupied by hookers and drug addicts—Bob's kind of people. Mom told me she hadn't given up on him and still prayed every night for Jesus to keep him safe. But he was away from her, and that was good.

In their second year apart, mom moved off my couch and into a tiny second-story apartment on 5th Street, diagonally across from Bethany Chapel. Before long she got a phone call—it was Bob and he was desperate. "The Motor Lodge kicked me out," he said. He had no money and was stranded at the Long Beach Airport.

I have no doubt Bob was penniless. Mom's credit cards were maxed out and his own credit was nonexistent. Whatever he did for money in the preceding two years had run its course—he'd taken one final trip on someone else's dime, and now he was forced to call up the *Big E* and beg for real. Mom took him in.

Bob behaved well after mom took him back. Her money and credit were gone so there wasn't much he could do besides take her back-and-forth to work, or cook dinner. Gone were the days of property ownership and San Diego hookers—now Bob just did whatever mom wanted, while taking the occasional flight back to Cleveland to visit family. Their big world had shrunk down, year-by-year, until they wound up in that little tiny apartment stall on the second floor. Mom liked that kind of life—she needed nothing more than that.

* * *

5pm. Bob pulls into the Postal Credit Union's parking lot, coasting his truck into an empty space. "She'll be out soon," he thinks. "I'll idle it."

The Postal Credit Union is not a building, but a large trailer made into a permanent bungalow. A long ramp takes clients up to the front door, which also serves as the employee exit. Inside, Elsie quickly counts bills to balance out her busy cash drawer—being the most popular teller comes with a cost. Her coworkers are done for the day, and head as a group to the front door. "'Night Elsie," they say in unison.

Elsie's attention remains fixed on her count, but polite words come easy: "Goodnight guys," she replies.

The door shuts behind the group, leaving Elsie alone and counting. She scratches down a final number and compares it to a second number: *Balanced.* Elsie smiles to herself—she's always been good at math.

The front door suddenly flies open and coworkers reappear. "Something's wrong with Bob, Elsie!"

Elsie snaps to attention, "What?"

"Come outside," they say urgently, "Something's wrong with Bob!"

Elsie hurries outside with her coworkers and hears Bob's truck revving full throttle. She rushes to the driver's window and peeks in: 65-year-old Bob Ireland slumps awkwardly over the steering wheel, dead from a heart attack.

That evening, the family—minus the Copps—rallied at Mark's house to comfort our grief-stricken mom. When I arrived, mom put me on the spot with a terribly unfair question: "Do you think Bob went to heaven?" Mom wanted the lie—tonight I was happy to give it to her. "Yes," I replied. She accepted my answer and sat in a quiet daze for the next few hours. No more questions were asked.

* * *

Inside Bob's truck was a carry-on bag for a flight to Cleveland he'd booked for the day after he died—that bag contained wallpaper and a roller. At the hospital, the contents of his pants were given to mom: A receipt for flower delivery, and the key to an LAX locker. The flower deliveries were for two different women: One was mom, the other was a lady named Kay in Cleveland. Even to the end, Bob was cheating on her.

Bob's Big Secret

We cared greatly for mom during this time but we had no sympathy for Bob. We hated him, and learning about his mystery woman in Cleveland was icing on the cake. However, the LAX locker key was extremely enticing since we'd always had our pet theory that he was a jewel smuggler. We wanted to find that locker ASAP, but first we needed to clean Bob's stuff out of mom's apartment. Contrary to everything else we did concerning Bob, this one was exciting—*Where's the jewels, big boy?*

The apartment search turned up nothing. Cheap watches, fat-guy blue jeans, and a closet filled to the brim with unopened boxes of laundry detergent. The hoarded detergent was weird, but Bob was weird—since he was a coupon clipper, we figured he bought them all on sale.

With the apartment a bust, Gilbert & Mark set off to LAX with Gilbert's son to hunt for the locker that matched Bob's key. Lo and behold, they found it. With a far-too-suspicious glance over their shoulders, the men opened the locker to reveal its contents—more boxes of *laundry detergent*. Mark grabbed a filthy airport pay phone to make a scratchy phone call to me: "We're coming back from the airport with Bob's stuff. Lay a tarp on the ground. I'll explain when I get there. [click]."

Forty minutes later, the boys arrived at my house with their haul.

"Laundry Detergent?" I asked.

"Probably how he gets jewels in without the dogs smelling it," someone replied.

My eyes widened. I remembered Bob's gift of *Colombian Emeralds* to me. The pawn shop said they were junk—maybe Bob kept the *good ones* for himself.

"Pour it out," I instructed the boys.

White powder poured from all directions as boxes were emptied onto the tarp. Detergent dust filled the air with the overpowering scent of clean clothes. A large mound formed itself into a pyramid on the tarp—somewhere inside lay Bob's secret. We sifted and scratched through the mound, feeling for anything hard. I pulled a peanut-sized clump of detergent and squeezed—it crumbled into nothing. Mark came up with a big egg-shaped clump—that crumbled too. We shook the empty boxes, listening for a rattle—silence. In desperation, we even took them apart. Just cardboard. Bob's locker was a letdown.

That was the mystery of Bob Ireland. Maybe he really went to Africa, and Colombia, and England, and more. Maybe he really smuggled jewels. Maybe I'm entirely wrong about him and he never set fire to my window; Or maybe Bob was worse than we imagined and left a trail of dead hookers up in the mountains. Nobody could ever figure him out. In the end, maybe Bob's detergent was just detergent —a final smirk from the grave.

* * *

Bob's funeral was a sad affair. He had no friends, so the only people there were a handful of Rasmussens and Irelands. Lana didn't attend.

Bob's son Junior was by then a flight surgeon in the Air Force, with a specialty in psychiatry. He had no nice things to say about his dad, calling him a strange man and summing him up in psychiatric terms. It was weird to hear, and must have been a punch in the gut having to eulogize a father nobody would vouch for.

In the 1970s, mom & Bob purchased four funeral plots (in a 2x2 stack) at the local cemetery. One stack was for mom & Bob, the other was for Anna—plus a wildcard plot for whoever wanted it. Mom once suggested that I could have it—an offer I immediately turned down.

Bob's casket was lowered deep into his grave plot, with space left above for mom. Decades later, we learned that Anna was already laying in the plot next to him. She'd died unannounced in the 80s and her corpse somehow traveled from Cleveland to California to occupy that plot. Anna Ireland and her strange son now slept together forever. *Mommy loved bananas.*

Part IV

The Copps

TERMINAL WIDOW

Mom accepted Bob's death far better than we'd imagined. She was certainly sad about it—expressing a desire to drive her car off the end of the pier—but considering the intensity of her previous dramas, this one was easy to manage. The biggest issue was figuring out where she would live. She still had her tiny apartment down from the church, but mom never liked being alone and we knew she'd soon make waves about it. We could have drawn straws to see who pulled the short one, but the contest would be pointless—Janice #2 was born with the short straw. Mom would live with me.

Two Working Women

My current home in Long Beach was already too small for my existing family, so adding another adult to the mix was impossible. A decent solution was found: Mom and I would combine incomes and move to a larger home in *El Dorado Park Estates,* a mildly affluent neighborhood with a rental home that fit our needs. Considering the Second Gary's physical state, those needs were great.

My second husband—named Gary, just like the first—was a self-employed graphic designer by trade whose favorite past-times were playing hockey and watching TV. Frustratingly, he spent far more time with hobbies than work. Throughout the 80s, I worked while he played. At decade's end, he became paralyzed after crashing his road bicycle into a parked car. After many months spent in rehab—with nurses who told me he was a great guy doomed by laziness—the Second Gary came home. He was perfectly capable of continuing work as a graphic designer—he was paraplegic, not quadriplegic—but work wasn't in his DNA from the start. Instead, he watched television in bed all day. At night, I'd come home from work to find him watching TV in the living room with his buddies. Nothing had changed with the Second Gary—no fire drove him to get working—in fact he'd only gotten worse. His disability checks were spent renewing the lease on a second-floor office he could never return to since it was only accessible by stairs. All financial responsibility—for family and for him—was placed on my shoulders.

A normal woman would have put her foot down long ago—even before his injury —but I was far from normal. The great personal strengths I learned under mom's rule—family loyalty and service to others—became faults when I found myself exploited and lacking a voice strong enough to be heard; Now that the Second Gary was paraplegic, service became exponentially greater while loyalty turned into a steadily tightening noose around my neck.

In that context, five people moved to our new rental home at 3440 Armourdale: Me, mom, two sons aged 13 & 21, and the Second Gary.

Christian Party House

Our large Armourdale house fast became the hangout for Rasmussen and Copp clans. My family—the Second Gary included—was always popular with Lana's kids, likely because we weren't really religious. We still attended their church, but with a critical eye and ability to inject humor that couldn't have existed in their homes—though Dave Copp was a witty man, Lana was humorless. The Second Gary's church-people caricatures on the back of tithe envelopes, together with Mark's critique of the newsletter's grammar, were otherworldly to the Copp kids. It was fun humor for my nieces & nephews, and even in my growing despair I enjoyed having them around.

Armourdale became the new base for Rasmussen & Copp holiday gatherings— events previously hosted by Mark & Debbie—and each successive holiday brought our families closer together. Aside from prayers before the Thanksgiving and Christmas feasts, religion was never discussed. In those moments, good times were had by all, but nobody knew what went on behind the scenes.

TIB

The Second Gary's buddies followed him to Armourdale, including Steve Schoch —stepson of Prophet David Schoch. Steve was a young divorced man who, despite his royal upbringing, was barely religious. He also played drums in Bethany Chapel's band. Steve and my husband hung out often—too often. After a year of the Second Gary failing to do anything to improve his (and our) situation, I voiced my frustrations with him. In return, he came up with a nickname for me: TIB—short for the *Take It Bitch*.

The Second Gary's nickname for me wasn't a private one—Steve also used it. It was a joke, used in front of me, at my expense.

The family portrait you knew was coming: Lana, Gilbert, Mark, and me.

There was no rectifying the situation or denying that I was, indeed, the TIB. I cooked for everyone, I paid for everything, and when my complaints were made fun of, I took the abuse. I was undoubtedly the *Take It Bitch*.

Cracks Form

The two incomes in the house (mine and mom's) were barely enough to make ends meet. Mom's mood swings weren't too bad anymore since Bob was gone, but she now used that extra energy to keep tabs on my behavior. If I missed church, she was right on me, demanding to know where I'd been.

My long-time girlfriends Lynn & Nancy were friendly with mom & the Second Gary, but they'd also heard my growing frustrations with them through the years. Concerned with my mental health, they invited me for a taste of the good life at *Phil Trani's,* a live music bar in downtown Long Beach. Trani's soon became my secret escape.

At this time I had serious dental problems, made worse when the Second Gary's leg spasmed one night and kneed me in the jaw. I visited a dentist who explained that my overall health was being dragged down by my broken teeth, and they needed to be fixed immediately. I relayed this to the Second Gary, and asked him for financial help from his disability payments, but he refused. He ultimately—begrudgingly —agreed to sell an old unused camera to help me, but it wasn't enough.

Meanwhile, my husband's buddy Steve—the Prophet's son—was making moves on me. The mighty Prophet David Schoch raised quite the man—one who entered his disabled friend's home to betray him and steal his wife.

Life at Armourdale became a cyclone. The Second Gary was shitting on me figuratively & literally—he sprayed diarrhea in my hair one morning while I helped him onto the toilet. His friend Steve was coming over to eat dinner with him, then staying for dessert. And mom reverted to the same one I knew as a teenager, demanding emotional support while also controlling my every move.

Armourdale looked great to outsiders, but inside was a woman on the verge of a mental breakdown. I wanted to scream until my lungs exploded—I had to get out.

New Year's Spanking

I finally cracked on New Years Eve, 1992. Bethany Chapel was having their annual candlelight service—an event as boring as it sounds—but I'd already made plans to hang with my girlfriends at *Trani's,* where the rest of the world partied. Mom saw me getting ready for the evening and questioned where I was going. When I took my stand, telling her I was headed to Trani's—*a live music bar*—mom's eyes fired up. She grabbed my arm, maneuvered around to my rear, and spanked me. I was 47 years old.

Shortly thereafter, I left the home. Fled. The Second Gary knew it was coming and wasn't happy. Others saw it coming, too. In my haste to save myself, I overlooked the other side of the equation: I forgot how vile Pentecostals can be.

A HOUSE DIVIDED

"I don't blame you," the Second Gary's mother told me. She knew her son well, and though she was a hard woman who rarely spoke to me, she was fair. To all the other people, of course, my fleeing was unconscionable. The *Take It Bitch* must forever suffer for our pleasure—or else.

Or Else

Knowing his father would neglect him, I took my youngest son to live with me and my new husband—a psychologist who promised to fix my teeth. That's when the true storm hit.

When it came time to vacate Armourdale, everyone *not named Janice* helped mom and the Second Gary move their stuff out of the house and on to their new living arrangements. Everything of mine was thrown out, including a big box labeled "Christmas Ornaments" that contained the little treasures my kids crafted in school. Gingerbread men, glittery cards, and hand-painted angels were trashed. Those weren't mine, they were my children's—cast aside and lost forever. The only people with that much spite were Lana and her meddling daughter, a 400-pound busybody who'd allied herself firmly with the Second Gary. That daughter —whose sinful secrets I kept private to prevent criticism of her parents' Christian message—wanted to burn me to the ground. How dare I leave *losers* and try to *win*.

If trashing my kid's Christmas ornaments wasn't enough, there was also Lana's written attack on me. I still had an office job, and one day I returned after lunch to find a letter from Lana on my desk. The only words I managed before putting it down were, "What will my kids do now that you're gone?" and the closer, "You're dead to me."

My sister Lana contained not an ounce of kindness. I never saw her initiate a hug or a kiss with a grandchild, much less her own children. A smile or laugh was always strained, as if it hurt to let her face do what came naturally.

Lana never struck me as religious—her participation in church was the bare minimum—but she was always very smart. As a young girl, she watched dad & mom spin their Jesus wheels for years without ever getting ahead. Seeing their failure, Lana figured out that the best way to make money with Jesus was through stability —by running a church.

Stability for Lana meant not involving herself with unstable people, of which mom was one. Her Saturday coffee with mom and Sunday *hellos* at church were temporary—mom came and went. With me out of the picture and Armourdale gone, mom was now living in a small cottage behind Lana's house. Even though Lana lived elsewhere—renting the big house to her meddling daughter—mom was still in a much tighter Copp-family orbit than before, and Lana hated me for it. That's the reason for her sudden grudge against me—that's why I was dead to her. To Lana, mom wasn't her responsibility, she was everyone else's responsibility—and everyone else meant *Janice*.

* * *

Over the next year or two, I had limited contact with everyone except Gilbert and Mark. I called mom once at the Credit Union to say hello and inquire about my account—she informed me that my account was closed due to inactivity, and *was there anything else I needed?* My gut feeling was that she closed the account on purpose—my punishment for defying the rules. *Another spanking.*

I was filled in on family life by my brothers, learning that many old-timers at Bethany Chapel had left after Lana's son took over and rebranded it. Mom hadn't left Bethany Chapel, of course—her loyalty to the Copp family was unwavering. Whether that loyalty was reciprocated never crossed her mind, though in the future it certainly crossed ours.

Mom's Phone Call

Around 1996, after things died down a bit, I got a phone call at work. It was mom and she was crying about my ornaments. It wasn't unusual for mom to cry, but it was odd that *she* called *me,* and odder still that the tears *weren't for her.*

Up until now, I had no idea that my Christmas ornaments were actually thrown out. I'd wondered aloud to my brothers where all my stuff went—including the ornaments—but never got any straight answers. Now mom was on the line explaining that my ornaments were thrown out accidentally, but she was crying about it.

For the very first time, I heard mom cry tears for someone else—that someone else was me.

Mom insisted that it was an accident, that my ornaments were left in a box on the curb and nobody thought to grab them—but I knew that was a lie. Knowing Lana and her bully daughter, I think nobody had the courage to stand up to them on my behalf. The last line of defense was mom, but she was powerless in the face of Lana and her bully daughter. Everyone drove away *knowing full well* the box marked "Christmas Ornaments" was left on the curb with the garbage, but only mom had a duty to save them for me. As a mother, she failed.

I believe this was the first time mom actually saw me as her daughter, *harmed*. And mom knew I was more loyal to her than anybody else, the closest thing she had to a mirror image—a woman who never took from people and always gave—and for that loyalty I was trashed. *Just like her.* That's why mom grieved on the phone that day. Though my ornaments could never come back, it was a turning point in my relationship with mom—a good one. I was now her daughter.

* * *

Another few years passed and the 90s turned over into the 2000s. I'd begun meeting with mom again on Saturdays, this time at *Polly's Pies* since *Clifton's* was long gone. Lana was there at first—she had no choice since she'd become mom's babysitter on Saturdays. Her 400lb meddling daughter joined us, too. Lana never said a word about the letter—there was no pulling me aside to apologize or explain herself. Her loudmouth daughter—always the first to talk—never mentioned my Christmas ornaments. I knew an apology would never come from them, but that didn't matter much to me—my purpose at those first Saturdays with mom was to get back in the swing of things. I was mom's true keeper.

The Copp Unit

With reconciliation came my reappearance at Mark's house for holiday gatherings, although these family events were much smaller since the Copps split off into their own isolated world. Bethany Chapel's trendy new incarnation operated best without Rasmussen baggage, and now that Lana's son Davey headed the family business, face time with the family *heathens* offered nothing but risk for him—we simply knew too much about him and the church. Every holiday brought the same Magic 8-Ball question: "Are the Copps coming?" and the Magic 8-Ball's answer was always the same, "Probably not."

Mother and daughter reunited

To be fair, the Copp family always made themselves available for mom, who was dead set on keeping us tied to them. There'd often be dual holiday parties, with mom transported between both. Sometimes the Copps actually showed up to Mark's house—always by caravan as a single large unit. Small talk abounded and new children were introduced, or reintroduced for older kids who forgot who the hell we were. The children might betray their parent's private conversations, like the time Davey's young daughter met me for the first time: "Oh, *you're the one*," she said to me. I wasn't offended because their feelings toward us weren't a secret. To quote what Davey's wife once said to a mutual friend, "They're the dirt side of the family." Yes, we know.

Not all Copps hold us in low regard. My niece Stephanie—who shares my middle name—has always been dear to me and never uttered an ill word. The same goes for other nieces and nephews, and even patriarch Dave Sr, who's always been pleasant to the Rasmussens. Unfortunately, the good Copps are overshadowed by the venomous ones who walk sideways to Jesus.

Another Elsie

At the age of 83, mom finally retired from the Credit Union in 2006. She was okay with retirement, but becoming quite sad about her appearance. Mom was a vain woman—she liked being the prettiest in the room—but in old age she knew those days were gone. She had a new church office gig working part-time with Lana and

Stephanie, and she loved Sundays at church where the young people worshiped her like a saint; Those things made her happy, but they weren't enough for a woman concerned with looking good. She also understood that her diminishing appearance meant a diminishing life, and she cried a lot to me about growing old. Mom still had her unreasonable gripes, but mostly she was sad about the future. It wasn't that her faith in Heaven faltered—mom was faithful to the core—it's just that she wanted to stay here forever with us.

Even though mom was known as Grandma to her grandchildren and others for decades, in her own eyes she was still Elsie. Upon realizing how others saw her, she discovered the fix for her depression. Mom came to terms with life as it was for her, reinventing herself as *Grandma Elsie* and opening her tender heart to the world. Her trusty coin purse frequently snapped open in church and elsewhere, revealing wadded bills that now flew beyond the usual family hands. Rewards came back to her in the form of birthday cards, smiling photographs, and warm hugs. By the late 2000s, mom knew more people than any person could possibly keep track of—especially at church where she was a celebrity. Whether the mostly young recipients were just in it for a buck didn't matter to mom: She was *Grandma* now—to all of them.

Undying Loyalty

Mom didn't understand what was being preached at the Copp's church anymore —the new codeword-filled sermons made her eyes cross—but she accepted it anyways. Elsie had blazed her own Jesus trail across the Midwest with Roy: two Christian pioneers saving souls and making babies along the way. If Davey's lightweight gobbledy-gook was the new spin on things, so be it. Mom's loyalty was to family, and as long as family had a church, she had a tithe envelope ready to lick.

Grandma's Cottage

After the disintegration of Armourdale in the early 90s, mom lived in a cottage behind Lana & Dave's home at 2527 Nipomo Ave. The home itself was occupied by the new owners—Lana's bully daughter and her bizarre second husband, a church hack who did handyman work for money. Other people came and went from the house: Missionary boarders, room-renters, even a foster kid—perfect for the meddling daughter to occupy herself with. All the while—as the main house ran itself crazy with instability—mom created a delightfully stable home in the rear.

The Nipomo property had a long driveway leading to a detached garage in the rear. Sharing a wall with that garage was mom's two-room cottage. Mom's front door opened into her little living room, where she slept on a couch made comfy with bedding. Each morning the bedding was neatly folded, and each evening it was relaid—mom was never lazy. The second room was slightly larger, containing a pullout sleeper for guests, of which mom had many. The second room had a tiny bathroom, but there was no kitchen—food was cooked in a microwave or on a hotplate stored inside a chest of drawers that doubled as a prep table. Milk and leftovers were stored in a mini fridge. At the rear of the second room was a nook hidden behind a curtain—that was mom's closet and changing room.

Mom's cottage was a place of maximum efficiency, created by a woman who knew better than anyone how to live poor. Grandkids stayed overnight on the pullout bed, and after our Saturday lunches at *Polly's,* adults convened at the cottage for coffee cake while breathing air tinted sweet by mom's outdoor rose garden. Of all the places mom lived, it was her favorite.

Hanging out in front of mom's cottage. All her rent went down the toilet.

As the 2000s came to a close, so did mom's cottage—Lana's daughter was losing the family home to foreclosure. Mom complained to me many times over the years about the loud outbursts coming from inside the main home, the husband's general weirdness, and her cottage being entered when she wasn't home. Mom was a paying renter with a right to privacy, as well as a grandmother owed respect. Neither of those things mattered to an obnoxious woman who intruded into mom's life whenever she saw fit. Besides rent, mom gave loads of money to her granddaughter over the years—at Lana's request. The foreclosure was evidence that all of it went right down the drain. After 15+ years of stability, mom was once again looking for a home.

Rossmoor Horror Show

Approaching 90, mom had no good options. She wasn't ill, she wasn't rich, and the rest of us weren't set up in homes that could take her in. She'd had a perfect arrangement—one that she paid tens of thousands of dollars for in rent—and now it was sunk. The only option was a bad one: use her good name to lease a home together with the 400-pound bully. This was a woman so enormous that she *broke a treadmill.* A woman who lost a remote control for an entire day *in her fat rolls.* A woman who misspent her grandmother's rent money, and more. Now mom was signing a lease to live inside a home with this woman and her weirdo husband. For once, mom's diarrhea was acceptable.

The house was located in Rossmoor, an affluent neighborhood sandwiched between Los Alamitos & Seal Beach that doctors and lawyers called home. Rossmoor's newest residents pulled the average down—way down.

Mom was extremely uncomfortable going into the arrangement; Once settled, her anxiety went through the roof. The granddaughter & husband were complete pigs, sleeping in recliners, never showering, and leaving full garbage bags that mom struggled to lift from the kitchen for disposal. Mom didn't have a room—those were saved for the *boarders*—so she slept in a little alcove off the main living room. Mom wouldn't have asked for a room, she might even decline the offer of one, but classy people know how to award things to those they respect; In this case, Rossmoor's lowest class had no respect for themselves, let alone their grandmother, leaving mom without privacy in a home that couldn't have been rented without her signature.

Stolen Prescription

The disrespect of mom reached new heights the day her happy pills were taken from her. At Mark's regular Monday-evening dinner with mom, she explained that Lana and the bully daughter confiscated her *Xanax* as they drove home from church the previous day. Now mom was stuck without the pills she'd taken *every day of her life* since dad died, and she was very rattled. Mark and his wife were outraged, not only by the disrespect but by the danger it created for mom: Lifetime users of anti-anxiety pills can't just quit them cold turkey. Mark & Debbie acted quickly, driving over to confront Lana's bully daughter and insist that she return mom's pills—otherwise they'd call the police. This, in turn, resulted in a phone call to me from Lana:

"Why is Mark giving us a hard time?" she asked.

"You can't take mom's prescription away, Lana. She needs her pills."

"Well, I won't have a drug addict for a mother."

"Lana, she's been a drug addict since we were kids. And it's illegal to take her pills—you have to give them back."

"Oh, I *should have known* you'd say that."

Click. She hung up on me.

Mark & Debbie got mom's pills back, but then had to return her to the Rossmoor home—the home she shared with her bully.

We don't know what sparked the sudden confiscation of mom's pills. Maybe the stress of the living arrangement caused mom to take too many and flip out in front of Lana. Maybe someone else in the house was stealing & abusing them, and the fix was to remove them entirely. Or maybe the meddling daughter woke up one day and decided to bully her grandmother around. The only thing we're sure of is that mother & daughter Copp confiscated an 89-year-old grandmother's prescribed medication and wouldn't give it back.

Change of Plans

The home was out-of-control and lease renewal was coming due—with nowhere else to go, mom would have no choice but to renew when the time came. Other people could do something about it though, and that's what happened when Lana's son Davey made a family-leadership call: His sister and her weird husband were being sent to South Dakota on sabbatical. Mom relayed to us the official purpose of the sabbatical—weight loss and marriage repair. Privately, we believed it was to protect the reputations of the Copp family and their church. Pastor Davey's sister was a never-ending trainwreck, her husband an untrustworthy buffoon. The faster these two obnoxious people were off the church scene, the better.

Davey didn't forget about the other party in this, and offered his grandmother a decent housing solution: Pay to build a new cottage behind his parent's house. Davey lived across the street from his parents and had lots of kids, turning Lana into a regular babysitter—something she didn't like, according to mom. Perhaps in Davey's mind, having another babysitter across the street was a win for all. You like babysitting *unruly little children,* right Grandma?

Mom had no other options, so regardless of her opinion on babysitting little kids (she didn't like it), money changed hands and the plan took off. To Davey's credit, he took charge and did what he thought was right.

The Many Faces of Mom

Mom wore many public faces throughout her life—most people do—but she also wore private faces around family. Her adult grandchildren got different looks, as did her children: Mark, Gilbert, Lana, and me.

Mom could turn her faces on and off like a light switch—sad mom would quickly become happy mom if she heard Gilbert was coming over. Her attention would also shift—mom would drop a conversation mid-sentence when the Copp's walked in the door at Thanksgiving. It was nothing personal—just a change of face for the better crowd.

If sadness is an indicator of honesty, then mom's face for me was most real. Mark also got an honest face. The face she wore for Gilbert was mostly a happy one, and the happiest face of all was reserved for Lana and the Copps—that face was supremely attentive, lighthearted, and *totally fake*. Mom's happy face showed who she respected most—those were the people she didn't want to let down.

Under Construction

While mom finished out the lease in Rossmoor, a crew of church people began work on her new cottage. Considering this would be the first time mom actually lived on Lana's property *with Lana there,* mom definitely had reservations about the setup. Lana was mom's jewel, but she had zero tolerance for mom's negative behavior—never had, never would—and mom knew it. It remained to be seen whether this novel arrangement would work.

Mom's stress increased as move-in day approached; That stress culminated in a *TIA* stroke. No rehab was needed—she still had full mobility and was able to care for herself—but it was a sobering reminder to all of us that mom was very old and needed more attention than before. Not a lot, just a little.

Davey's church gang ultimately did a splendid job on the cottage, turning 150 sq-ft into a liveable space with thoughtful extras like safety handles in the bathroom. All of us were jazzed for mom's new digs—all of us except mom, who was very nervous. She expressed to me a concern that she might open the front door and disappear down the sidewalk—the same sort of disappearance threat she'd made to us as children. My response was predictable: I stayed with her that first night, sleeping on the floor while she took the trusty old couch. In the morning, I reassured mom that everything would be fine, then I left on a Vegas getaway.

That evening I received terrible news: Davey's kids went across the street to visit *Grandma* and found her lying on the floor—she'd had a major stroke.

Get Out

Mom's stroke was a bad one, requiring six weeks of rehab to teach her how to use a walker. She moved and spoke very slowly now, and it was obvious she'd need a caregiver from this point forward. Mark & I went to the cottage to discuss a plan forward with Lana & Dave. In our minds, the four Rasmussen kids could pool their money to coordinate help for mom at her spiffy new residence—the one she paid to build.

We arrived to learn a decision had already been made—Lana told us directly that mom could no longer live there. She walked out and was replaced by Dave, who explained that mom was concerned about "walking down the sidewalk and disappearing," and they couldn't do anything to prevent that.

Mom didn't have dementia, so there was zero concern that she'd wander off; Even if she did, how far could she get with a walker? Having gone there with Mark to coordinate a caregiving plan, we were left dumbstruck by Lana's announcement.

Dave's comment betrayed the true issue for Lana: Mom's threat—the same one she wielded so painfully against three of her children. Lana escaped those threats, fleeing the house at seventeen to marry Dave. Now she got her first taste of what mom did when she landed in someone's home, and she reacted accordingly—*get out.*

I believe mom dreaded the reality of living with Lana. The idea was good in theory, but how could it ever work in practice? Mom spent her entire life repeating the same controlling behavior, from suicide threats to diarrhea Saturdays to crying for an audience at the kitchen table. Working with Lana in the church office, or going to Copp-family lunch on Sundays, was a far cry from living full-time on Lana's property, and her nerves had already acted up—that's why I slept on the floor that first night.

Mom's behavior around the Copps—her happy face—was always an act, and she knew deep down that it couldn't go on forever. She also knew damn well how Lana treated rejects. When the whole charade eventually came crashing down, mom would lose the face she prized most.

Though mom's walkout comment could have been errant or anxiety induced, perhaps it was a subconscious means to torpedo the whole arrangement—to save her from herself. Or maybe it was a gamble for control that backfired. Regardless, Lana's no-drama line in the sand had been crossed, and the caregiving discussion for mom never happened. Elsie Ireland—age 90—was no longer welcome at the cottage she paid for.

Who's Taking Mom?

The rest of us scrambled to figure out mom's next destination. Mark's house had no room and too many steps, Gilbert lived hours away from church, and I lived with my son's family which gave me no control over the home. We still couldn't fathom Lana's behavior towards our stroke-ridden mom: What would the church think about their holy Copp matriarch if they learned she kicked out an old-lady renter whose money was good? What if they found out the lady in question was saintly old Elsie Ireland—everyone's twinkly-eyed grandma who never missed a Sunday or a tithe? Once again, Bethany Chapel threw a widow to the dogs.

Mark and I visited mom in rehab to ask her directly where she wanted to live. Her answer was no surprise: *I want to go with Janice.*

Thankfully, my son and daughter-in-law welcomed mom with open arms. There was great history between my son and his grandmother—they'd cohabitated for a year or so in mom's Nipomo cottage. He was her champion and she was his. My daughter-in-law also excelled at respect for elders: If her house had room, why wouldn't she welcome grandma to live there?

Together Again

We got mom sorted into a spare bedroom at my son's house. The stroke left her in terrible shape, reliant on a walker but extremely unstable while using it. Her speech was also very slow. We purchased a hospital bed with rails so she wouldn't fall out, and setup a little television so she could watch the shows she enjoyed— *Jerry Springer* was her favorite, plus *Lawrence Welk* and the *Christian Broadcasting Network*. My always-attentive son labeled her remote so she knew exactly what buttons to press. Lana's contribution to the mother she kicked out was the bare minimum: she and Dave showed up one-time-only to bring mom a fan, then left after five minutes. I know Dave would have stayed longer to chat with mom, but Lana ran the show.

A Challenging Time

All things aside, mom was happy with the arrangement. Mark & Debbie were a huge help, picking mom up every Sunday to take her to the church that didn't want her. Gilbert, who lived further away, was unstoppable as always, regularly driving the hour or two it took to visit his mom. Mom loved Gilbert's visits— she'd often remark at how much he reminded her of Roy.

There were immense challenges though. Mom needed simple meals (that Mark helped with), but she also needed service of those meals. She had pills to take but needed assistance opening the bottles. Bathing was impossible at the house, so we paid a lady from the church to take mom for a bath once a week. The biggest challenge, of course, was the bathroom. We tried a commode chair over the toilet, but it was too messy and mom didn't like imposing on her grandkids. The solution became my own personal horror show: we placed the chair over a bucket in mom's bedroom.

Mom knew full well what was happening and insisted on paying for carpet cleaning because of the mess, though my son and his wife never gave it a second thought. The indignity of the bucket bothered mom greatly—she was a classy woman used to paying her own way. As the bucket dumper, it bothered me too.

The Talk

After a year with the bucket, mom began falling during the transition from walker to commode chair. She was basically dead weight, so when my son wasn't around it was nearly impossible for me to pick her up. Mom and I both understood what that meant—she had to enter assisted living.

I sat in the bedroom with her and explained why she needed care beyond what I could provide. Mom knew that it was too much for me—that she was dragging me down with her. We cried together, then mom put her brave face on for me: *"Okay, I'll go."*

My brothers and I found a facility near the house so I could visit mom every day and make her feel part of us. She'd have a little room that we could decorate how she liked, yet she'd be taken care of by professionals. It was a good plan, but mom was scared and rightfully so—she'd be living with strangers.

Mom kept her brave face on while moving to her new home, but I could see that she was very sad. Mom was 91 years old and knew life was ending. Family and friends regularly visited to surround her with love and attention, but mom was alone in spirit and heart. She still made it to church through the kindness of Mark and others, even though her valiant effort wasn't reciprocated: She cried to me that Pastor Davey—her grandson—never visited to pray with her. Mom still paid tithes to his church, and she knew Pastor Davey visited other shut-ins—so why not her?

Lana's Turn

While mom was at Meridian, Lana suffered a stroke of her own. The first stroke was followed by an additional one, ultimately leaving Lana bedridden in a nursing facility. I visited Lana there—she had no idea who I was, and wouldn't make eye contact with me (or anyone else for that matter). She was in awful shape—yelling profanities, speaking in tongues, and accusing the gardener of trying to have sex with her. It was a terrible state for Lana that I wish I'd never seen.

Since Lana's condition was so bad, mom never had a chance to visit her—something that bothered her greatly. Mom knew the end was coming for Lana and there was nothing she could do to stop it—her daughter couldn't be saved.

<u>Sister with a Steel Spine</u>

Lana never spoke about early family life. She was the oldest child and had the most time with mom & dad, but whenever we questioned her about it, she wouldn't budge. Not a word about it—ever. I thought it was extremely selfish of her.

Lana would hate me writing about our family. She'd call me on the phone and bark hurtful words to make me stop, because Lana wanted it all to be a big secret —she had nothing to gain and everything to lose by having our Pentecostal history laid bare.

I spent decades making small talk with Lana over coffee and pie, and that was exactly how she wanted it. I should have been braver with her—we all should have been—twisting her arm a bit at *Clifton's* to insist she answer our questions. But would it have mattered? Nope. Lana was indifferent to us because she quite simply didn't care: We were three, she was one, and that was that.

<u>Are You Ready, Grandma?</u>

Mom spent Christmas Eve 2014 just like old times, together with us at my son's house. The Copp family asked if they could join the party, which thrilled mom to no end. She put on her Copp face and awaited their arrival—in the giant Copp caravan, of course.

The Copp family arrived without Lana, who remained in a nursing home. Once again, we went through the motions of reintroducing the children, and introducing new ones who'd spawned since our last meeting. Adult cousins joked with their counterparts, and Dave Sr's witty self provided warm laughter and innocent kicks. But Davey—mom's absent Pastor—committed the party foul of the century when he pulled a chair up to speak with his grandmother:

"Grandma, *are you ready to see Jesus?*"

The shocking question took me a few seconds to process. My daughter walked out of the room, followed shortly by myself; We convened in my bedroom and cursed this doofus and his idiot question.

When the night came to a close, Mark and I took mom back to Meridian. She cried in the car—the blissful joy of a warm family gathering spoiled by Pastor Davey's cold reminder that it would be her last. It was so terribly hard to leave mom alone in her room that night.

* * *

On January 22, 2015, I received a text message from Lana's meddling daughter:

"Hi Aunt Janice, wanted to let you know that our mom passed away today and is residing with Jesus."

I phoned Gilbert and Mark to let them know. We planned to tell mom together, but when I visited her that day she could see something was wrong and inquired what it was. I told her Lana died and hugged her. Mom said she was very sad. I was too.

When Gilbert and Mark showed up, we explained how Lana languished for two years in a horrible state, and that it was much better now that her suffering was over. Our conversation lasted a few hours until we all left, exhausted. I'm sure mom cried alone in her room. We cried too—whatever the cold history, Lana was one of us.

Another Pentecostal Funeral

Lana's funeral was held the following week at Davey's church. The sparse church used folding chairs instead of pews, so seating could be configured however deemed appropriate. Two sections were set up for the funeral: A section for us, seated directly in front of the service, and one for Davey's small congregation, set up perpendicular to our left. That meant they all looked straight at us, while we looked straight at the service. Considering the barely religious nature of our gang, we must have appeared like bizarre zoo animals to the Pentecostals observing us. The few old-timers remaining from Bethany Chapel days—the ones who didn't leave when Davey changed formats—greeted us warmly. Everyone else just stared.

We brought mom to the funeral in her wheelchair and she held up well. The service was respectful, aside from a pre-recorded eulogy submitted by Davey's owner—a pastor based out of Trinidad & Tobago—who remarked that Lana once *got on her knees* in front of him out of respect. He also made an odd joke about Lana's tiny feet.

After the weird pre-recorded eulogy, live action kicked off in the church as the Pentecostals screamed in tongues like monkeys in a rainforest. I couldn't take it and went outside; Gilbert was already there. We'd heard more than enough tongues for one lifetime—it was nonsense noise from nonsense people.

I knew the funeral would be bad for mom. When I went to Meridian the following day, her nurses said she was very down and kept saying she wanted to be with her daughter. I knew mom was giving up.

Peaceful Days

I wanted to make mom's last days as good as I could, so I'd bring in colorful little knick-knacks to spark up her room—she lit up every time I brought them. I managed to get her old pal Eunice in for a visit, too. They laughed about the insanity of life with their husbands at Minneapolis Bible School—of that curtain they hung in the bedroom to separate Lennings from Rasmussens. The good old days.

Mom and I had many wonderful conversations in our time together at Meridian. When I suggested she go to Vegas for a lost weekend indulging her wild side, explaining that it would broaden her horizons when it came to men, mom had a big laugh. That's how it always was in our closest moments—I'd say the things mom couldn't. She liked when I got angry with people and sweared, and if the mood hit right, she'd skirt the rules by joining in with Norwegian curses of her own—then stop herself and have a big laugh. I helped mom tap into the side of her personality she loved but couldn't live.

Mom was always guarded about life with her father, but she let slip a memory of herself in Alfred's lonely home, playing piano and daydreaming that one day someone would find her and love her. And that's exactly who mom was—a lonely little Norwegian girl wanting to be loved. Wanting to belong.

Elsie's dream was realized with Roy—true love from an honest man. Once he was stolen away, that little girl was back in Alfred's cold home, playing piano for anyone who would listen.

Mom told me many times that I was like a mother to her, that she could always count on me. I never liked it, asking, "If I'm your mother, then who is mine?" Mom laughed off my question, but she was right: That lonely girl playing piano never had a mother until she had me. Mom knew I'd always listen, and she knew we were in it together—mother and daughter to the end.

Mom wouldn't agree with how I tell her story, especially when it comes to the church. She'd say I was too tough on Jesus and Roy, and insist I be nicer to Andy and Bob. She'd be unhappy that I curse Alfred with my hope that he's drowning in bitterness inside his frozen South Dakota grave. Exposing David Schoch as a false prophet (and a terrible man) would make her very upset. Bethany Chapel and the Copp family would be completely off-limits—no matter how true my criticism, my words would horrify mom. But her wild side would *love it.*

* * *

Mom tried to be happy for me, but her twinkly smile was gone now and she was very fragile. She still made it to church on Sundays, courtesy of a warm-hearted woman named Doris, but on mom's final trip she was unusually quiet and distant.

We held mom's 93rd birthday at Mark's house. The Copps didn't show. She sat on the patio listening to our conversations—mom loved hearing family talk—but she didn't join in much. Mom laughed when we suggested a plane flying overhead was going to sky-write a birthday message, but I could sense her sadness in knowing it would be her last birthday. A month later, on June 18, 2015, staff at Meridian found her unresponsive and transported her to the hospice next door.

I went to her immediately and knew she was dying. I spoke, but she never opened her eyes. Visitors from church came by to see her. My daughter came to sit with her, as did her cherished grandson Tim—who held her hand so very sweetly. Her other grandson—Pastor Davey—was missing in action when she passed. I'm glad she died without knowing that.

<u>Funeral Insult</u>

Mom's intense loyalty manifested itself in pride at having never been divorced. For her, the loyal thing to do was rest with the man to whom she'd lasted vowed an oath. That man was Bob Ireland, and her coffin rests atop his. Mom's true love—Roy—remains alone in Costa Mesa's Veterans Cemetery.

We had a simple gravesite service for mom. Bob's kids attended, as did a few young Credit Union coworkers on whom mom made a lasting impression. A few church people came, but their leader didn't show. The only Copps attending were my lovely niece Stephanie, and Dave Sr—who officiated per our request. They would have attended anyways.

Pastor Davey's new-age church offered no service to the woman who'd spent a lifetime pouring money into it. Instead, the grandmother who knew better than anyone what faith meant was crammed in as an afterthought to a Sunday night service. The Rasmussens weren't invited—our knowledge of it came second hand. If there's a Norwegian curse word for that type of behavior, I'm sure mom knew it.

* * *

The last time I spoke to mom was no different than any other time, except I could see that her energy was very low. By then I'd learned to hug and hold her deeply— to impart my physical warmth and love. I made little jokes for her benefit and she smiled at them, but we both knew she didn't have many days left. When our visit came to an end, I got up to leave and told her I'd see her tomorrow. As I exited the room, mom's weak voice reached my ears with the best gift she could ever give —something she'd never said to any of us before: *"I love you sweetie."*

EPILOGUE

Elsie Ireland Interview w/ Tim Rasmussen

Meridian Gardens Assisted Living | Anaheim, California

April 2, 2014

In April of 2014, my grandmother Elsie Ireland was just shy of her 92nd birthday. I arrived at her assisted living facility at 12:30 PM, the day before my own 41st birthday. Grandma was in the community dining room, eating at her table alone. She immediately perked up once she saw she had a visitor. I joined her, and over the next several hours I asked questions about her life and her past—questions about family lore I was interested in and knew would soon disappear forever. I wrote her answers in my notebook as fast and accurately as possible. The family's mileage may vary as to the veracity of her answers, but grandma that day wasn't shy about talking about any of the matters below. The following is a lightly edited transcript of my notes from that day.

Memories Of Growing Up

Ole Thompson (her grandfather) would read to/tell young Elsie stories from Zane Grey, which she loved. She said he walked from Wisconsin to South Dakota for his land. He worked the grain elevator in Bruce and walked four miles into town every day. Years later, at 93, he was cutting down some trees (his favorite pastime) and one fell on his leg. He said he didn't want to live anymore if he couldn't cut down trees and died shortly after. She says she couldn't go to his funeral because she was living in California at that point.

As a kid, she remembers Calvin Coolidge came to Brookings. Young Elsie had whooping cough so her aunt hid her under a tree. In those same years, she also says she was on a train ride once and a man approached her father Alfred and said, "$10,000 for your little girl."

She spoke of her mother Therese dying. Said her dad kept a trunk of Therese's belongings upstairs. Elsie and her siblings were never to have it. Her brother Harold was eight years older than her and had memories of their mother Therese. He told grandma their mom studied music, was beautiful, but other than a single uncle who occasionally visited, the Amlunds never came to visit after Therese died. Harold said the Amlunds were high class and probably felt Alfred, as a farmer, was too low class. Grandma never knew what happened to that trunk or what was in there. She thinks her dad was too heartbroken to ever talk about it.

After that she lived separately from Harold and sister Thelma, who were taken away and raised by other uncles. It was rough on her because she felt completely isolated. Harold was handsome and grandma called him "Dimps" due to him having one dimple. But they never really talked because they didn't live together. She said when Roy died, she vowed to keep her kids together because she knew what it was like to grow up alone. She says Therese is buried at Deer Creek Cemetery/Church and that Mark has a box with Therese's obituary in it.

Grandma remembers being a chubby kid and walking back to her Grandma's house from town. Elsie said to her dad, "Dad, I'm so tired…" and Alfred picked her up and carried her the whole way back. She knew from that he loved her. Decades later, Alfred was on his way to see grandma and died in Tucson. As an adult, grandma never asked him about his late wife/her late mother. She just knew not to talk about it with him.

On The Rasmussens

She said Grandma Rasmussen (Roy's mom Matilda) was so tiny and cute, had white curly hair. Elsie said she likes clowns because of living in a small town. The carnival would come to town and clowns would "make us laugh." Also hobos. She remembers sitting on her porch with hobos (who were well-dressed and came in on box cars on the train), and Grandma Rasmussen would tie up a blue handkerchief with three days of food in it. Grandpa Rasmussen (Roy's dad Gilbert) was a big man and kind to her, speaking Norwegian. He never signed a note [loan] for anything. Said his word was good and everyone knew it. Grandpa Rasmussen took care of four brothers and each of them had a plot of land. He watched over the Lenning cousins because a few of them were drinkers. She said Grandpa Rasmussen was kind of like a policeman. Everyone answered to him and he was a smart, wise man. Every time a family or a woman lost a husband, Grandpa Rasmussen would just build another room on the farm and they'd move in. She remembered her first night visiting the Rasmussens. She was sitting at the table next to Roy's brother Herman who turned to her with a glint in his eye and said, "And what do you think you're doing here?" At the Thompson house they were strict at the table and there were never any laughs, very European. At the Rasmussen's you could laugh and do anything you wanted. She said during the Depression, Herman's wife's mom was Maddie Walters. Maddie had a cow and she milked it for food, which kept the whole family going.

Elsie's Wedding Day (circa 1940)

She said her and Roy's wedding was at Grandpa Rasmussen's farm. Her sister Thelma made her wedding dress. After the ceremony, Roy's sisters-in-law Phyllis and Lorraine cooked. They had a "luxurious" dinner of mashed potato, home-made rolls, pickles, and cake. Grandpa Rasmussen gave Roy and Elsie money for their honeymoon in Waterston, South Dakota (about 40 miles from Bruce). They probably borrowed Grandpa Rasmussen's new Chevy or Ford to drive there. Their honeymoon lasted one night! They stayed in a beautiful hotel. "Can you imagine what that meant?" I playfully remarked, given their strict religious upbringing, they were both presumably virgins on their wedding night so, "How did that go?" Grandma smiled and said everyone seemed to know what they were doing.

On Working After Roy Died

She worked the night shift at the post office for five years, that's where you had to start. She worked the 6 PM – 3 AM or 7 PM – 4 AM shift. A day shift finally became available but grandma wasn't there so a sympathetic supervisor slipped her name under the door for consideration and that's how she got it. She said Janice cooked and raised the kids. She was 13. One time Mark told grandma that he was "tired of dancing," which didn't make any sense. Mark finally explained Janice wouldn't give him ice cream unless he danced for her. When asked what would've happened had Roy lived, grandma thinks they'd have moved back to the Midwest at some point. The reason they went to California in the first place was Laurel wrote a letter to Roy that started, "My Dear Baby Brother Roy…" and that's all it took for Roy to follow.

On Her Decision To Be Buried With Bob Instead Of Roy

She said at the time of Roy's death the Veteran's Administration offered her a plot next to Roy, but the cemetery in Costa Mesa in 1957 was new and basically just a cow pasture. She said, "Whoever could've thought it would build up the way it has over the years?" When asked about Roy, she says she thinks of him a lot. Bob, too.

On Andy Taylor

Grandma said she dated Andy for ten years and he always had other girls. Andy used to accuse her of going out behind his back. Grandma says she had so many men wanting to go out with her they could never figure out why she ended up marrying Bob. Andy's ex-wife went to Bethany and the church got into Elsie and Andy's business because of that. Andy said of himself he was a cad. But then in seriousness, he said he'd force grandma to take a lie detector (re: other men) and it scared her. At the post office, the vets all had jobs and were tough. They'd throw piles of mail on grandma's hands. Andy would bring lunch/dinner to her. She'd cry and he'd say get up there and be tough and quit crying. She says Andy was the only reason she survived at first. And he loved her kids.

What Attracted Her To Bob Ireland?

She smiles and says, "He was nice to me and had a Ford Mustang. He was always trying to give me a ride (from the post office window)." When they would go out to dinner, the waitress would come up and ask for drinks and Bob would answer, "This young lady and I are too young to drink." Grandma said he was smooth.

On Learning Bob Was Still Married The Night Before Their Wedding

She shrugged and said, "I never thought about it really. I don't know why." She said he was good to her sister Thelma, took Thelma to the hospital and doctor appointments, gave her a thousand dollars.

On Bob's Womanizing

"I was plain dumb." She always suspected but didn't say anything to him. She said Bob would do mail then clean stuff at night. One time she saw his ex-wife hit him at a restaurant. She said Bob had probably said something not nice. (Grandma said she was raised strict Lutheran and could never hit or tell someone to shut up). She said one time Bob went to Israel with minister Rex Humbard's church and she didn't hear from him for days. Bob's mom and sister were going to come the next day and grandma was planning on calling the police/missing persons. Bob eventually told her what he did. Grandma was going to leave him but Thelma begged her to stay because Thelma wouldn't have a place to live. Grandma said it seemed like Bob had two personalities. "Bob got harder after retirement." Bob Jr. begged her to leave, begged her to not let Bob handle her money. Grandma said she doesn't regret any of it. "His dad was hard, German. His mom Anna was sweet to him." At 15, Bob had to drive a fruit truck. Said his mom's full name was Margaretha Diedrickson and grandma always loved that name. Grandma said of herself she was a small town girl who didn't know anything about men and had no one to talk to.

More Questions

I asked her, "What's the worst thing that happened in your life?" She said the worst thing was Roy dying. He was popular, charismatic, kind, everyone loved him. They lived in one tiny room but always had company. They would unfold the beds and since there was no floor space they'd crawl from bed to bed. Elsie always cooked for all the visitors. Roy took care of the cars of the President of General Mills and also the head of the symphony orchestra.

I then asked her, "What's the best thing that happened in your life, besides me showing up today?" She smiled and said, "That's one of them." She thinks awhile and says "singing, as a kid, even though my childhood was tough." She starts crying at the memory of a little Norwegian plate with a prayer on it. She didn't speak English until going to grade school. She loves Norwegian but doesn't know why she didn't teach her kids. She had a hard life as a child but has fond memories of certain moments and especially that language. She doesn't remember what she wore to church as a kid, but adults would pinch her cheeks and say in Norwegian, "snill," which meant you were sweet and a good girl.

Grandma said when she was little it was "so cold in dad's house at night." She would sleep on the wooden kitchen table next to the stove. Her dad and Harold slept upstairs, and dad wore a stocking cap and long underwear. At 14 or 15 she started "cussing to be a big shot" and Alfred looked at her and said, "What's wrong with you? Don't you know English?"

On Regrets

Grandma wishes she could have kept some of her properties because they're all gone now. She says her biggest regret was not taking advantage of three scholarships she got after graduating high school, but that she didn't have any money for living expenses at college. One time she went to talk to a banker on her own but chickened out because she was too timid. She wishes she wasn't such a rule follower all her life. She regrets being so timid, even though she says she was a strict mother because, "There's five of us, someone has to run it."

On Dying

I asked her if she thought about dying and she said, "Every day." She worries about dying. "I want to be with and live with my family, to go on living with them." She remarks she still calls to make sure the cemetery puts flowers on Bob's grave (which she wants for hers). She thinks back to earlier decades: "We were so poor but so happy. As long as we could go to church and play Rook." She said just the day before she'd overslept and then broke down crying because the kitchen had closed, which was the first time that had happened to her. Then Mark appeared and tapped her shoulder and said come spend the day with him, which was music to her ears. I ask if she's ever doubted her faith. She says she's never doubted it, but it still doesn't comfort her in old age. "Two and two don't always make four."

After more than two hours of reminiscing, I wheeled grandma back to her room. I joked (since she mentioned missing her job at the credit union so much) that she should set up a TV tray in her doorway with a cash drawer and make change for the residents. I kissed and hugged her goodbye. Long past were the days when she'd slip me a $20 bill and then fuss about me fussing about it. She died a year later, age 93, the same as her grandfather Ole.

Janice Rasmussen was born pissed off in Hoven, South Dakota. She currently lives in Long Beach, California, with Georgie—her faithful canine companion. Janice has three children and two grandchildren.

—

Ron Johnson is a Long Beach native residing in Boulder, Colorado, with his wife and two dogs. Ron's hobbies include listening to music and gardening.

Other work by Ron Johnson
Televangelist
Lunch Special
How to Grow Organic Cannabis
The Jim Bakker Foodbucket Fanpage
Black Room Productions (YouTube)

www.ingramcontent.com/pod-product-compliance
Lightning Source LLC
Chambersburg PA
CBHW030247130626
46549CB00002B/427